PRAISE FOR *MESQUITE*

"By turns informative, playful, funny, and wise, *Mesquite* is a fascinating, tour de force illumination of the natural, cultural, and spiritual value of a truly remarkable desert tree. Gary Nabhan's gift to readers is the imaginative and redemptive suggestion that we still have plenty to learn from the more-than-human world that flourishes even under the harshest conditions. A gem from one of our finest western American writers, *Mesquite* is a spectacular accomplishment and a wonderfully entertaining read."

—MICHAEL P. BRANCH, author of
Rants from the Hill and *How to Cuss in Western*

"With a reverently irreverent blend of natural history, magical realism, social commentary, and humor, Nabhan invites us to fall in love with one of the America's most misunderstood and maligned plants. Masterfully performing the great sleight of hand trick of classic nature writing, Nabhan employs close observation of the outside world to go deeper within."

—LIZ CARLISLE, author of *Lentil Underground*

"In this rapturous, provocative, and intimate book, Gary Paul Nabhan takes readers on his quest for symbiosis with mesquite! It's a paean to the venerable desert legume, a humorous meditation on human knowledge, and a somewhat Kafkaesque journey into the deep state of vegetal oneness with a tree. It is full of wry observations, heartfelt hopefulness, and vivid stories – with a big dash of trippy fun!"

—COURTNEY WHITE, author of
Grass, Soil, Hope and *Two-Percent Solutions*

"It seems that Gary Paul Nabhan has been experiencing a case of mesquiten identity! In this book we learn how he came to belong to the genus *Prosopis*. Along the way we also learn about mesquite biology, evolution, ecology, culture, cuisine, and conservation. Like the mesquite, Gary is deep-rooted in our arid landscapes and communities. He crosses borders. He bears blossoms of wit and pods of knowledge. As he finds himself transformed, so does the reader. We become a bit more mesquite-like ourselves—and, somehow, that much more human."

—CURT MEINE, conservation biologist,
senior fellow, The Aldo Leopold Foundation

"Delicious! This book nourishes the soul, home, and palate with stories and characters as alluring and complex as the trees they love and celebrate."

—BRAD LANCASTER, cofounder of Desert Harvesters;
author of *Rainwater Harvesting for Drylands and Beyond*

Other Books by Gary Paul Nabhan

Ethnobiology for the Future

Food, Genes, and Culture

Growing Food in a Hotter, Drier Land

The Forgotten Pollinators
(with Stephen Buchmann)

Gathering the Desert

The Desert Smells Like Rain

Mesquite

An Arboreal Love Affair

GARY PAUL NABHAN

foreword by PETEY MESQUITEY

CHELSEA GREEN PUBLISHING
White River Junction, Vermont
London, UK

Project Manager: Alexander Bullett
Project Editor: Benjamin Watson
Copy Editor: Nancy Bailey
Proofreader: Rachel Shields Ebersole
Indexer: Deborah Heimann
Designer: Melissa Jacobson

Printed in the United States of America
First printing August, 2018
10 9 8 7 6 5 4 3 2 1   18 19 20 21 22

Our Commitment to Green Publishing

Chelsea Green sees publishing as a tool for cultural change and ecological stewardship. We strive to align our book manufacturing practices with our editorial mission and to reduce the impact of our business enterprise in the environment. We print our books and catalogs on chlorine-free recycled paper, using vegetable-based inks whenever possible. This book may cost slightly more because it was printed on paper that contains recycled fiber, and we hope you'll agree that it's worth it. Chelsea Green is a member of the Green Press Initiative (www.green pressinitiative.org), a nonprofit coalition of publishers, manufacturers, and authors working to protect the world's endangered forests and conserve natural resources. *Mesquite* was printed on paper supplied by Thomson-Shore that contains 30% postconsumer recycled fiber.

Library of Congress Cataloging-in-Publication Data
Names: Nabhan, Gary Paul, author.
Title: Mesquite : an arboreal love affair / Gary Paul Nabhan ; foreword by
    Petey Mesquitey.
Description: White River Junction, Vermont : Chelsea Green Publishing, [2018]
    | Includes index.
Identifiers: LCCN 2018019460| ISBN 9781603588300 (hc) | ISBN 9781603588317 (ebook)
    | ISBN 9781603588270 (audiobook)
Subjects: LCSH: Mesquite. | Ethnobotany.
Classification: LCC QK495.M545 N33 2018 | DDC 583/.633--dc23
LC record available at https://lccn.loc.gov/2018019460

Chelsea Green Publishing
85 North Main Street, Suite 120
White River Junction, VT 05001
(802) 295-6300
www.chelseagreen.com

I speak of the tree in mind,
its foliage our language.
Do you ask me for an answer?
I have none. I know only
that the tree is ourselves, different
as the instruments of an orchestra
are different, but without which
the symphony is incomplete.

R. S. Thomas, "The Tree,"
Uncollected Poems (1981)

. . . at home as the year's seeds begin to fall
each one alone each in its own moment
coming in its blind hope to touch the earth
its recognition even in the dark
knowing at once the place that it has touched
the place where it belongs and came to stay
this is the place that I wanted to hear . . .

W. S. Merwin, "Ripe Seeds Falling,"
Garden Time (2016)

crying along the trail
packing her cradle board
"Hey woman, you dropped your burden!"
"No . . . I buried him in a tree."

Jaime de Angulo, "Shaman Songs,"
Home Among the Swinging Stars (1974)

Dedicated to my Mesquiteer Mentors:
Ivan Aguirre, Juanita Ahill, Jeau Allen, Martha Ames,
Esperanza Arevalo, Molly Beverly, Stephen Buchmann,
Tony Burgess, Alberto Burquez, Vince Kana'i Dodge,
William Doelle, Richard Felger, Hugh Fitzimmons,
Ed Frederickson, Art Garcia, R. Roy Johnson, Brad Lancaster,
Dennis Moroney, Petey Mesquitey, Cristina Monroy,
Laurie Smith Monti, Mark Moody, Carolyn Niethammer,
Juan Olmedo, Clifford Pablo, Amadeo Rea, Sunny Savage,
Amy Valdés Schwemm, Humberto Suzán Azpiri,
and Raymond Turner

CONTENTS

FOREWORD

I was a kid from northern Kentucky seeking adventure when I first arrived in the Sonoran Desert. The application to attend the University of Arizona was easy, and Tucson sounded pretty cool, especially in Kerouac's *On the Road*. But within minutes of getting off the airplane at Tucson International Airport, I came to the realization that I was in a foreign land. I couldn't even pronounce the name of my dormitory. I still owe a thank you to the cab driver who patiently gave me a Tucson tutorial as we headed to my new home at the Kaibab Huachuca dormitory. "That tree with green bark is called a *palo verde*. That's Spanish for 'green stick.' Oh, and now those tall cactuses with arms . . . those are called *saguaros*. Pronounce it right. Nothing worse than folks getting that wrong. You're gonna love it here."

Well, not right away, but yeah, he was right. I mean, I was a far cry from the grassy pastures and junglelike hardwood forests of my youth. So it took a year or so, but somewhere in that period, something happened. I'm not sure I can point to an event or an epiphany, but I do remember going home to Kentucky over a school break and wanting desperately to get back to the desert. I was captured, and I've never left the borderlands since. Oh, I tried a couple times, but no, I came scurrying home to the desert.

And so for the last fifty years, I have been educated by the borderlands and its occupants. Many of the occupants that took me into the fold were the native plants and animals and, yes, the occasional human. You hold in your hands the work of one of those humans.

MESQUITE

As a grower of native plants, I remember trying to simply get folks interested in sense of place. "Native plants remind us of where we live," I'd say to folks. And it's true, but there is more. There is history and stories that come with our native plants, but is there any more interesting story than that of our native mesquites? As I read Gary's book, I caught myself muttering, "right on," "oh yeah," or "I'll be darned, I didn't know that." There were a lot of those moments, and as I read on I had my love of mesquite not just confirmed, but renewed. Oh my goodness, Gary, you rascal, I am a Mesquiteer!

So you are about to go on a marvelous mesquite journey filled with stories that will sometimes have you belly laughing, sometimes have you thinking maybe you're working on your thesis, or maybe even striking a chord that makes you quietly weep . . . okay, maybe that's just me. But one thing is sure: When you've turned that last page, I suspect you will be a member of the Sacred Order of Unconditional Lovers of Mesquite Trees. So come on, turn the first page. Mesquites are waiting for you, and they're beautiful. Yeah, they are.

PETEY MESQUITEY
Near the banks of the Ol' Guajolote

Arboreality

I am here to convince you that you may have never fully seen, smelled, heard, tasted, or been touched by a tree. In particular, I humbly submit that you and I have yet to fully fathom what a tree can be . . . or at least, what a mesquite tree can be to us. If we can concede that this may be true, there is the very real possibility that some tree can become a beacon for each of us, a luminous life to guide us on our wayward journeys. It can shine a light on how we should live our lives.

Now, don't get me wrong: I am not putting down your or anyone else's observational skills, intellectual acuity, or affection for a species other than our own. Indeed, you and other folks I know may have deeply studied a tree's shape, sampled its fruits, measured its yields, or admired its colors and textures and flavors.

But few of us have come to grips with the many nuances of what it means *to be a tree*. There are so many unexplored dimensions, hidden attractions, and intangible values associated with the Woody Ones of this Wild and Woolly World. This is especially true when we consider what the reality of trees might be like in the "deepstate," or what forester Peter Wohlleben calls *life's lower story:*

> We only know a tiny fraction of what there is to know about the complex life that busies itself under our feet. Up to half

the biomass of a forest is hidden in this lower story. Most life-forms that bustle around here cannot be seen by the naked eye.

That is why I fear and fret that we have grasped no more than the most superficial aspects of *arboreality*, the experience of being a tree as it truly makes sense of this world around us. A tree is not just another pretty face. It is a sentient being of consummate poise, sessile grace, and impeccable instincts. It has the capacity to care for us, *to love*. We might do well to become more like these towering, flowering kin of ours.

I do not pretend to have been any more cognizant of this fact over most of my life than you have been over yours. In fact, I am embarrassed to say that it wasn't until quite recently that my own staid manner of viewing trees was forever shattered as a result of a mishap that shifted my perception. That psychic shattering was what prompted me to write on the wood pulp that you hold in your hands or the more ethereal stuff you hold in your digits.

I don't mean to sound confessional, but there's nothing to brag about with regard to what precipitated my breakdown.

Not long ago, I was thrown off-kilter and suddenly brought to my knees by a bout of dizziness and nausea. I could not immediately diagnose whether it was a case of vertigo, of influenza, of the sixty-seven-year itch, of the great political malaise that was afflicting much of America, or of an unprecedented rupture of my former identity.

This illness ravaged me while I was wandering through one of the great hyper-arid landscapes of the Americas—Organ Pipe Cactus National Monument, which stretches out along the US–Mexico border like an iridescent mirror reflecting the essential desert in each of us.

Over several horrifying hours, I could not stand up even for a moment without falling back onto the earth. I could not look up without seeing the world spinning violently around me, and I could not open my mouth without disgorging my innards. And so I slid back against the only thing behind me that would prop me up enough to keep me breathing. Otherwise I would have expired.

INTRODUCTION

As I slumped against some unseen object that steadfastly kept
me from sinking farther into the earth, I looked up just long enough
to see limbs wildly waving above my head, bending to embrace me.
And then I passed out.

When I awakened, I had no immediate recollection of where I was
or how I had gotten there.

I felt unspeakably *disoriented* in every sense.

After a few minutes of feeling completely abandoned by everyone I knew and everything I cared about, I caught a glimpse of the
only clue in sight that might reorient me to my whereabouts, what-
abouts, and who-abouts.

Next to me—under my left elbow, in fact—was a small metal
placard that was stuck into the hard, dry ground on a stainless steel
spike. The placard simply said these words:

MESQUITE
PROSOPIS VELUTINA

I began to entertain possibilities of what this placard might
mean for me, to me, and about me.

Was it plausible that I had begun to metamorphose into a mesquite tree?

Might it be that my torso had become thickened and torqued
into a somewhat twisted trunk?

Could it be that those limbs I had glanced at were *my* limbs?

Oddly, I felt drained of all humanity, ambition, and *volition*. It
was as though I had lost my capacity to walk, run, or become mobile
by any other means.

And yet, for whatever reason, I no longer feared becoming *sessile*, which is to say, "rooted in place." I no longer had any urge to
"get away," to "go it alone," or to retreat to "someplace else."

Still, it was not as though I had become paralyzed, as if I were
unable to be moved by the beauty of the world. As I glanced upward,
I saw those limbs—*my limbs?*—genuflecting, then reaching upward

3

toward the heavens, with all my leaflets reverberating in rhythm to the slightest stirring of a desert breeze. The leaflets were gradually turning to track the rays of the sun; they folded up close with the first signs of drought; and they opened up again in response to the merest hint of rain.

Whenever phainopeplas landed among the mistletoes attached to my limbs so that they could eat and then defecate the berries of that hemiparasitic growth, my branches bowed with gratitude. Whenever floodwaters reached my roots, I could feel them swelling with pride in their capacity to store moisture. Whenever my blossoms burst open, I felt a pleasurable tingle as bees worked my anthers and pistils, sipped my nectar, and shook my pollen until it burst loose.

I was, for a minute, an hour, or an afternoon, *in arboreal rapture*.

And then, rather unexpectedly, I heard a woman's voice whispering to me:

"Are you alright?" she inquired.

I could not immediately speak; I moaned, I was in such ecstasy.

"Me and the hubby over there . . . well, we've been watching you from our wooden bench over yonder for nearly an hour, and we've hardly seen you move at all. Are you sick? Or stuck? Or stoned?"

My throat felt choked up with something thick, like sap. I tried to bark out a few words, but I could not be sure that they could be heard:

"Not sick. Not stoned. *Sticked*. Stuck. *Lovestruck*. I've been kissed by the love bug."

She looked over her shoulder and waved to her spouse.

"He's making noise now, honey, but he ain't making much sense . . . I'm sure he's alive, but I am not sure he's kickin' . . . or that I understand what he's trying to say . . . or sing . . ."

I tried again with all my might to sound rational, but instead, these few words went warbling out of my mouth:

"I once was lost . . .

But now I'm found . . .

Was blind, but now . . .

I'm tree."

Of course, rapture seldom lasts forever, but whatever had rather unexpectedly happened to me that day in the desert seems to have rewired my life. My arteries now flow like xylem and phloem; my toes and soul reach deeply into the soil.

Like many of you, I had heard at different points in my life how lovers have come to live as one; how saints became one with God; and how hermits gripped by the naturalist's trance become one with nature.

Although I had fleetingly felt such oneness, I didn't know exactly how to rekindle those feelings so that their very warmth could and would stay longer within me.

And so I did the only thing I could think to do when facing such a dilemma.

I decided to apprentice myself to a tree.

Not to any tree.

To a mesquite.

I chose to spend a year with mesquite as my guru and guide, my teacher, my preacher, my lifeline, and perhaps as my lover.

The stories that follow are what I learned along the way: how to greet a tree, how to eat a tree's bounty, how to be sheltered, loved, or healed by a tree, and ultimately, how to be a tree.

You too might aspire to participate in one of these pursuits. That is why I am inviting you to come along on this desert journey into arboreality.

You may someday need a change in habit and habitat as much as I did.

CHAPTER ONE

Nurses

I must concede, it was initially hard for me to admit to others—even my wife—that I felt as though I was becoming a tree, or at very least, becoming one with a mesquite. I worried that I might have been possessed by a mesquite spirit or that I had suffered from a fungal infection by some mutant mycorrhizae that were slowly transforming my toes into rootlets. In the weeks following my breakdown in Organ Pipe Cactus National Monument, I'm sure that my wife, Laurus nobilis (sweet bay), realized that I was undergoing some kind of change, though she never inquired directly about it. But I'm sure that she noticed the litter of leaflets and sap I left in our bed after a restless night of metamorphosis...

In order to give her a hint of the transformation I was going through, I suggested to her that it might be interesting for us to get to know the mesquite trees in our neighborhood a little bit more intimately, since they outnumbered the human residents in our area a thousand to one.

Laurus, in turn, suggested that we go out together into the desert for a morning outing to harvest mesquite pods. There, in a heap of those mesquite pods, lies the seeds of this love story. It soon became clear to me that both the mesquite and my wife had a thing or two to teach all of us about desert living.

"Wait a minute, you ol' Tree Doctor, you," I heard her say. "Just what do you think you are doing? I know desert rats like you and your buddies think you are old pros at harvesting mesquite pods, but lookie here . . . watch how I am doing it. I'm letting the *tree* tell me which pods I should take . . . "

I glanced over my shoulder to catch a glimpse of my wife, Laurus, and began wondering if she had just gone goofy with sunstroke. We were out early one Sunday morning in July, already glistening in the desert heat as the sun blazed down upon us, and the rocks beneath our feet began to bake the bottoms of our shoes.

But no, Laurus had not been "touched" by the sun nor hit by dry lightning. She was waving for me to come over and carefully watch what she was doing.

"See? I'm not *pulling* or even *picking* the pods off the tree; *it's giving its ripest ones to me.* It will tell me which are those that are ready to eat by whether they've reached the point where they can drop off the branch on their own accord, or whether they're still hanging on tight. Listen to what the tree is telling us . . . "

At first, I heard the tree buzz with bees. Then I heard a white-winged dove chant its mantra, *"Who cooks for you?"* before taking flight from the other side of the tree's dense but feathery canopy. Next, I heard a few pods drop to the desert floor on their own from a branch above me.

Then, when I simply brushed my fingers across the other pods still poised on the same branch, they virtually leapt into my wicker basket on their own, detaching from their little stems with hardly any pressure or pull.

As usual, my wife was right.

I had not been deeply listening to the tree, nor observing the gifts it was freely giving to us.

I had been off in the clouds.

———————

Now that I was back down on earth, I took a good look at the pink-streaked pods, each holding a dozen or so seeds in their sweet pulp. I placed them in my wicker basket, and then glanced over again to look at the pink-lipped lady standing next to me.

No wonder I was in love—not just with this tree, but with the girl who stood beside me beneath its canopy. I had met my match in this herbalist, this nurse, this Border Healing Woman, who knew how to listen to the sound of one mesquite tree clapping.

In response to that timeless philosophical query, "If a mesquite tree falls in a desert forest and no one is around, how can we know if it made a sound?" I am sure that Laurus would hear it—she is so attuned to mesquite trees and their sounds. (I was in luck, should my metamorphosis continue.)

I could see by her outfit that she was a *mesquitera,* a veteran mesquite pod harvester. She donned a long-sleeved but lightweight shirt and gloves to protect her skin from the ever-present thorns hidden along the feathery bunches of foliage into which we were reaching. She wore short-legged pants of the kind we used to call "pedal-pushers," made of fabric tough enough to endure anything that pricks, sticks, stinks, stings, or clings in our Stinkin' Hot Desert homeland.

Laurus had been trudging along in ankle-high boots that could protect her pretty little feet from any tumbleweeds, rattlesnakes, and red ants that happened to cross her path. And her blond hair was bundled up under a broad-billed Mexican sombrero that was strung around her neck tight enough to keep any prankster tree from knocking it off when she walked under its limbs.

In addition to these fashionable accoutrements carefully selected for pain-free desert living, Laurus carried her own stylish wicker basket. It was already full of freshly picked pods that she would clean, dry, grind, sift into fine flour, and ultimately grill into mesquite waffles.

Yes, I was still in love with my waffley-wedded wife, but both of us were also in love with the shapely mesquite that loomed large on our horizon that day.

Call us a "tree-some," I don't care. Having one of the three of us deeply rooted in this desert place offered the possibility that the other two of us might eventually get rooted as well. In our society, it appears that rootedness has already become a "nesting behavior" that most humans of this millennium have forgotten how to practice. We have instead become a nation of noodling nomads, restless and rootless rounders, if not tenacity-impaired tumbleweeds.

But before my mind itself wanders off again, let me return to my point: *To love a tree is not an offense;* it is the little-practiced expression of affection and respect for the wildness and woodiness of the world. And don't accuse me of any illicit *arboreality,* because it won't stand up in court. The glee that Laurus and I express in the presence of a mesquite tree is both wholesome and healthy.

In any case, mesquite tree hugging is the kind of sin that the world may need more of. In fact, the desire to love and be loved by a plant—at least ones other than carnivorous plants—may not be a sin at all. We are simply talking about biophilic affection and interspecific gratitude, nothing more.

Indeed, such close encounters with the photosynthetic kind may be a necessary reminder that our lives are as fundamentally dependent upon the sunbeam-transforming miracles of the plant world as they were on our mother's milk when we were mere babies.

To be sure, those of us who dwell in or near the Stinkin' Hot Desert are not promiscuous types; we pledge our allegiance to the mesquite and the ancient desert forest landscape in which it stands.

The mesquite is to us what the bison has been to the Plains Indians, what salmon is to those who live along the Pacific North Rim. It is most definitely our ecological, cultural, and metaphorical *keystone species.* For millennia, mesquite has been of paramount significance as an unfailing foodstuff, as a beverage, as a nectar source for honeybees, as a medicine, as a symbol or icon, as an antiseptic, as "material prima" for architects and artisans, and as a source of fiber and fuel for all comers.

In our neck of the woods, the singular importance of mesquite has outstripped the combined importance of corn chips, cell phones, aspirin, ammonia, plywood, beer, bungee cords, and charcoal briquettes for desert living.

Taste and see: Mesquite-smoked steaks from beeves browsed on mesquite leaves and pods! *That's what for dinner.*

Mesquite tortillas curled up and crammed full of sautéed squash blossoms, chopped-up cactus pads, and bite-size bits of chiltepín peppers! *That's what's for lunch!*

Mesquite waffles, with mesquite-blossom honey slathered all over them. *That's what's for breakfast!*

Over the years, I have eaten so many meals of mesquite that the molecules in my body have already voted in favor of me becoming a tree.

You may not have previously pondered it, but this tree is clearly what has nourished bazillions of desert rats over the last eight millennia out here in the mesquite-studded, cactus-punctuated, snake-rattled landscapes forming the gritty core of Arid America.

These days, Laurus and I happen to live in a small rural village called Patabutta, Arizona, on the upland bridge between the two biggest and boldest deserts of North America—the Sonoran and Chihuahuan—where mesquite savannas and grasslands form what I call Our Home on De-Range.

Patabutta happens to be within spitting distance of the US–Mexico border, where drug runners tunnel under our yards like giant sand worms, fly over our rooftops like cocaine-carrying vultures atop ultra-lite planes, and speed down our dry washes like roadrunners being chased by Wile E. Coyotes.

On a clear day, we can see the pollution in the border towns, and it too carries the smoky fragrance of mesquite. Especially on cold winter mornings, we can see and smell plumes of mesquite smoke rising up from the makeshift chimneys, corrugated stovepipes, and grease-stained grills in the shantytowns, *barrios,* and *colonias* of Nogales, Sonora.

During the winter, mesquite warms our skin, our throats, and our bellies. It is the preferred firewood for fireplaces and barbecue pits all across the North American deserts.

I am not typically a whiskey drinker, but when an arctic surge dips desert temperatures down below 80 degrees Fahrenheit, I have been known to partake of a delectable mesquite-smoked antifreeze from Hamilton Distillers called Whiskey del Bac, if only for survival's sake.

Other than my wife, Laurus, the mesquite tree is the only other resident of Patabutta, Arizona, that I affectionately call "honey." In the spring, mesquite's fragrant flowers offer nectar to many kinds of bees, one of which then transforms it into a fragrant amber honey.

Our friends Kara Schneider and Jaime de Zubeldia have kept some of their top-bar hives by the little pond on our property.

Their bee colonies are hidden away in the shade of the mesquite *bosque* just below our straw-bale house. The bees waggle-dance their way up from our pond, where they can drink year-round, and into our mesquite groves, hedgerows, orchard, and gardens, where they can collect nectar and pollen. Jaime and Kara kindly provide us with enough honey from their hives so that we can ferment herb-infused mead to offer to the desert druids who hide out beneath each densely branched mesquite tree on our property.

That's right: desert druids. While most of America is awash in Smurfs and Zombies these days, we prefer cohabiting with a band of desert druids. They are the guardians of the mesquite forest. They threaten to kick the butts of all bulldozer-driving, chainsaw-wielding, herbicide-snorting nozzleheads who senselessly try to mow down any of the mesquite trees in our valley.

Now, don't get me wrong: I am not "agin" the pruning of mesquite trees nor against those who wisely use their wood. I would not disparage anyone who harvests or selectively removes particular trees. But few of the folks I've met have ever really needed to eliminate an entire patch nor clear-cut whole swaths of them. This senseless slaughter makes plants-rights activists sizzle.

There's a big difference between giving a tree an annual haircut with pruning shears and slitting its trunk with an ax or a chainsaw. I usually do the pruning just before the pods come on in early summer, or again in late summer, just before a second flush of pods ripens in early fall. This is to allow us to offer a mesquite tree a full-body embrace when Laurus and I go out to gather the honey-colored pods from mesquite trees scattered all around Patabutta.

After we fondle all the foliage until the pods just fall off into our hands, we rest for a moment in postharvest bliss. We then dry the pods out in the sun or toast them in tumblers originally designed to roast chile peppers.

The pods begin to blush after all this stimulation, their sweetness exuding from every cell. That's when we know they are ready for consumption, or as we call it, "consummation."

We grind them into a sweet but savory flour that we serve for breakfast in a variety of ways: *tamales, panqueques, atoles, pinoles, moles,* and Bulgin' waffles. And when we serve our friends a plateful of such mesquite-laden morsels, they often eat them while sitting on our chairs constructed of mesquite, before a 6-foot-long table of 2-inch-thick mesquite board, sighing with pleasure.

Mesquite does not merely nourish our bellies; it also frames our view of the world from our outpost in Patabutta. When I awaken on a summer morning, I amble out to a dining room where I can glance out at a panorama framed by the mesquite trees just beyond our windowsills. The hummingbirds, orioles, and finches at our bird feeders are already up for the day and using those mesquites as their roosts and nesting grounds. Cottontails and pack rats are already nibbling on the golden pods scattered beneath the trees, having them for breakfast. Mesquite is like a golden bell that rings and clangs at dawn to awaken all the lives in the desert to the possibilities of the new day. "Wake up, honey," I hear it call out to me.

When fall arrives, the mesquite leaves begin to drop from the trees' canopies, as chilly mornings and lingering drought reshape the frame they make. Their deciduousness allows sunlight to hit the walls and windows of our home once again. I gather up the branches heaped on the ground beneath the trees and cut them into the kindling we use all winter long.

The kindling gets staved into the fireplace in our living room and in our beehive-shaped *horno* on the patio just outside the kitchen door. In that wood-fired oven, mesquite smoke imbues the flatbreads we bake, the game birds we roast, and the vegetables we grill. When placed on our barbecue grill, chicken breasts dusted with mesquite flour become *pollo asado ahumado con el sabor del mesquite.* Quite a mouthful, huh?

I've even used mesquite smoke to season sea salt gathered from the shores of the Gulf of California, the hypersaline body of water also known as the *Mar de Cortés.*

But those are not the only ways that mesquite trees refresh, sustain, and comfort us. I often sit on a stool hewn from mesquite boards while Laurus and I are filling corn husks with mesquite-flavored tamales or shredding jicamas and cabbage into mesquite-glazed coleslaw. Sometimes, we go outside and do such work on our porch, under the mottled shade of a half-dozen inter-twined canopies of mesquites that also encircle our rain garden of medicinal herbs. These shade-loving *yerbas medicinales* seem to thrive in the feathery shadows of these nurse plants, or *madrinas.*

Yes, *madrinas,* the word my Mexican neighbors also use for the godmothers of their own children. They also use the term *nodriza,* or "nurse," to describe a tree that offers a caring embrace and protective cover in an otherwise harsh, austere environment. The irony of that latter term was not lost on Laurus when she suspended her career as a nurse practitioner to gain a PhD as an ecologist of *nodrisismo* (nurse plant ecology). Her dissertation elaborated on the nurse plant ecology of mesquites and ironwoods, which provide sanctuaries for more vulnerable medicinal plants that grow under the protective canopies of these trees.

Now, Laurus may be the only nurse practitioner in the world who graduated from taking care of human babies to mastering the practice of interspecific nursing of baby shrubs and cacti. She under-stands that the desert forest may be shorter than most, but it still needs trees like mesquite and ironwood to "mother" the others.

Under the skirts of these two mothers, most of the aromatic herbs, thorny cacti, slinky vines, sumptuous shrubs, and fleshy suc-culents begin their lives in desert landscapes. They provide the "dark gaps" under which other plants sprout and survive as seedlings, just as most life in the rain forest begins in "light gaps." Mesquite and its distant kin in the desert bean family—palo verde, palo fierro (iron-wood), catclaw acacia, feather tree, and mimosa—are not only mothers, but also midwives, godmothers, nurses, chaperones, and sponsors for the other plants of the desert.

You can hear these relationships in Spanish names like *madrina, nodriza,* and *madre-cacao,* ancient terms of endearment and meta-phors for the protective embrace of particular tree species like mesquite. They suggest that the trees are "offering sanctuary." Per-haps such terms make sense only if you are truly *familiar* and *conversant* with the qualities of the tree itself, as if you are in an intimate relationship with it. Given that hundreds of thousands of Latin Americans have spoken with such intimacy about mesquite, tepemezquite, huisache, kapok, guamuchìl, or palo fierro, perhaps Laurus and I do not deserve to be called weirdos or sickos when we express our own love for mesquites.

To be sure, there is something touching in this notion that these trees are caring for you, sheltering you, and protecting you from stress. It does not matter whether you are a night-blooming cereus cactus, a wild chiltepín bush, a wolfberry, or a fallible, flaw-fraught human being: These elderly mesquites are there to offer you unconditional love, or at least, a shelter from the storm.

And mesquite indeed has weathered all kinds of storms—meteorological, ecological, cultural, and political. It has somehow gained the tenacity and perspicacity to *stay put,* remaining in place even when everything else in the landscape around it seems to be shifting. What I mean by *staying put* is this: Mesquite has an extraordinary capacity to survive in place and even thrive under all sorts of adverse conditions.

———

What I've begun to sense is that even if I don't fledge fully into treehood, perhaps this arboreal way of looking at, living in, and loving the world might help me and the rest of our own frail species learn to be more resinous, resonant, *or* resilient. *That is, if we even allow ourselves to become mesquitelike, to be guided by the prophetic* Prosopis.

What I am now wondering is whether mesquite is more than just a protector and a nurse, whether it has truly become my mentor or my lover. To be sure, it has felt its way through living here among many of our neighbors longer than we have. For us to fathom how the mesquite has managed to do so, we might first wish to understand how other peoples have spoken (with obvious affection) of this venerable tree. We need a vocabulary of intimacy to speak to a lover. So let us begin to learn how to speak this loving tongue.

CHAPTER TWO

Words

As I felt this desire to overcome the limits of my own humanhood—surrendering to the desire to become one with mesquite—I sensed I needed a fresh language. I needed a deeper, more detailed, and more sensuous vocabulary to express my admiration and affection for this tree, something more than:

> Oh, those shapely curves, those sinewy limbs, that tantalizing torso of a trunk . . .

While I admired the mesquite's shapeliness, I also sensed that if I might be on the verge of learning to feel, taste, see, and listen to the world as deeply as the mesquite tree itself does, I might love its kind more wildly and intimately. Humans obviously use a language to communicate with one another in a manner different from how trees communicate, with their chemical cues and electrical signals, their responsiveness to touch, sound, smell, and light.

Nevertheless, I was still human enough to feel it was worth remembering a few of the words that this tree itself has heard over the centuries, as humans have stood in its shadows, admiring it, flirting with it, caressing it, or gossiping about it.

These terms of endearment have helped sustain eight thousand years of love affairs among the forty-some species of gnarly trees in the genus *Prosopis* and our own gnarly species, *Homo proto-sapiens.* For those of you who use Latin only as your second language, the latter term means that we are the "not quite wise guys" at this point in our evolution. The Latin term *prosōpis* is an ancient name once given to the bristly burdock plant, the Velcro of the Old World. Like mesquite does here, the burdock holds its world together . . .

I guess you could say that the term refers to any plant that clings to you—or that you cling to. And oddly enough, the Latin term might be derived from an older Greek noun, *prosōpon,* for "face." Thus, *Prosopis* can be understood as a lover with an unforgettable face, a lover that holds you tight.

Let me be clear about one thing from the start: To know such words with regard to the mesquite is not enough to fully know the tree itself. *You must know it in the flesh.* For just as secondhand gossip often veers away from the physical truth, words alone can never really reveal all the sensuous dimensions nor deep heart of a mesquite, let alone tell of all its adventures from seed to shining tree. Carnal (or vegetal) knowledge is really the only way to go.

And yet, the indigenous lexicon regarding the dimensions of "mesquitivity" reveal to us one very significant sensibility. Many of the words linked to *mexquitl*—the ancient Nahuatl term for mesquite —remind us that many lives exist *in relation* to this tree. They occur as extensions of it, and not as separate entities.

These beings are like flocks of birds that roost, breed, nest, lay eggs, hatch, and fledge hatchlings out amid the branches, as well as eat of the fruits of the tree, all the while filling their mouths and their lungs and their bellies and their cells with the essence of mesquite. They are as much a part of the tree itself as its florets, branchlets, and rootlets. While not technically the same genome or melody as *Prosopis* flowers, foliage, or phloem, they are the harmonies in the love song swirling about it.

Some phrases of that love song have altogether ancient origins *and* have stood the test of time. So let's learn a bit of that pillow talk between intimates.

As I hinted earlier, the most commonly used names referring to the forty-five species of tree legumes in the genus *Prosopis* are mesquite and mezquité. They are derived from the Nahuatl word *mexquitl*, which originally stood for two particular mesquite species found in the semi-arid Altiplano and Valley of Mexico—*Prosopis juliflora* and *Prosopis laevigata.*

But alas, not long after Cristóbal Colón began the Great Colónoscopy of the Americas, this term became Hispanicized as *mexquité*, and then as *mesquité*. It then went viral, so to speak, entering American Regional English by 1805, although it was sometimes spelled simply as *mesquit.*

And as the tree and its uses spread, the M-word also spread all the way around the world in a matter of relative milliseconds compared to the ancient origins of mesquite trees way back in Tertiary times. We now speak of *honey mesquites* (a term of endearment, of course), switch mesquites, bull mesquites, velvet mesquites, and screwbean mesquites with the same familiarity that we speak of jack pines, jack-in-the-pulpits, and desert jackalopes.

But let us remember that other names for *Prosopis* remain in common currency: *acatín, algarroba, chachaca, chúcata, ghafh, haas, jand, kui, taco,* and *tahí*. Most of these are primary terms—what linguists call "unanalyzable lexemes"—that suggest they are ancient terms of endearment. We will return to these *abodos,* nicknames, pen names, pet names, *prestanombres,* and *noms de plume* in a while.

Now here is where it begins to get interesting, if not downright *mes*-merizing.

The mother term, *mexquitl,* gave rise to a host of luscious descriptive terms that provide us with hints into the intimacy of the interactions between humankind and mesquite-kind.

I have always loved the Spanish word for mesquite woodlands: *mezquital,* pronounced "mesquite-all." It is derived from the Nahuatl term *mexquitlah,* an *arboleda,* bosque, forest patch, grove, wooded habitat, or stand of trees displaying a stunning abundance of mesquite! Perhaps this ancient term reminds us that mesquite is less a solitary individual and more a glorious manifestation of "all our relations" present in this otherwise dry and sometimes lonely world. Mesquites usually party together, engaging in veritable orgies of life in ways that elicit envy, jealousy, and even outrage among more Victorian vegetation types.

And so my Mexican friends typically identify any prolific patch or fecund forest of these trees as a *mezquital* or *mezquitera*. But *mezquitera* can also mean a woman who nurses along, labors with, or makes products out of mesquite, just as a *mezquitero* can be a man who does the same. Thus, humankind and mesquite-kind are wedded by such words.

As in any particularly playful partnership or lovemaking activity, it is good to be rather specific about the anatomical terms relating to your partner. With regard to mesquite, these are quite detailed in some indigenous languages, and for good reasons.

While collaborating with the Seri or Comcáac foragers and fishers who live along the Sonoran coast of the Sea of Cortés, Laurus has learned dozens of anatomical, morphological, and developmental terms for mesquite in their endangered Cmique Iitom language. According to our ethnobotanist friend Richard Felger, these include descriptive terms and names for the flowers, for the pinnate leaves, for eight different developmental stages of the pods, for the loose-textured flour and the coarse fiber of the pods, for the smooth seeds and the hard exocarp "shell" surrounding each one, for both the inner and outer bark of the roots and the six kinds of cordage woven from various combinations of them, for two kinds of gums or resins, and for two kinds of wood, each useful for different kinds of construction and elaboration of crafts.

If you are to be a truly attentive partner, you've got quite vocabulary of intimacy to draw from, huh? *The Joy of Sex* can offer no better lexicon—I guess you gotta learn every nook and cranny of the tree, every stage in the sexual play of its flowers, every motion and moan.

But there are also names we must learn for the various kinds of nourishment provided from the mesquite tree, just as we must learn the many ways to care for and "nourish" the various needs of our lovers. The intimacy of eating and being eaten are embedded in these terms.

One of the oldest may be *mezquitatol,* a bubbly *atole* or fermented beverage made by crushing and soaking the pods in cold water in a clay pot inoculated with naturally occurring strains of desert yeasts. It has been likened to a sweet but mild beer by the Pima or O'odham of Arizona, who called it *o'oki navait* and probably used it ceremonially to bring down the rains. While it does not maintain its yeastiness for very long before bacteria make it sour, it does offer a nice buzz for four or five days.

A thousand miles north of the Nahuatl heartland, the sugary pods used for such beers are called *péchita,* a term apparently derived from the Opata word *péchit,* a word that jumped from central Sonora to be used over a much wider area. The term *péchita* is now known by indigenous and immigrant dwellers in the Sonoran Desert on both sides of the border and is probably more widespread than what borderline Anglos awkwardly call "mesquite beans." Beans they are not; they are pods.

A second indigenous food product made from the ground pods of a mesquite tree is a tamale called the *mezquitamal.* Its subtly cinnamon-and-coconut-scented *masa* has the sweetness of carmelized turbinado sugar, like that derived from cane stalks freshly mashed on an *trapiche* of two stone mortars sliding over one another. The taste of a *mezquitamal,* my friends, is to die for, without a doubt.

Still another specialty is a pale, cream-colored gum that exudes from wounds on the trunk of the tree. It hardens into a crystalline resin still traded into a few regions of Mexico under the Mayan name of *chachaca.* It is chewed as a snack by children, but it is also widely used like Murine or Visine as eye drops to remove obstructions beneath eye lids. This desert medicine for dust-filled eyes is more widely known as *mezquicopal,* a Nahuatl term derived from *mexquitl,* for the tree, and *copalli,* for a gum, resin, or incense.

There is more. An additional medicine of fame in the pharmacopoeia of many Mexican families is called *mezquitina.* It is an alcohol-based tincture derived from an infusion of mesquite leaves.

Now, just when Laurus and I thought we had mastered the lexicon of loving a mesquite tree, a conversation with our Mexican friend Juan Olmedo reminded us of another treasure trove of mesquite-related terms. They were first recorded on paper and translated by Bernardino de Sahagún, a Franciscan brother who arrived in New Spain in 1529.

As a Franciscan myself, I have been amazed at how many terms for mesquite one foreigner recorded throughout the Nahuatl-speaking communities he visited, not just in the palaces of the Aztec Empire. I'm even more amazed that such a massive lexicon for mesquite was compiled by a foreigner who *was* a Franciscan, since most of us in this order are recognized for our wanderlust and not very well regarded for meticulous scholarship nor for data organization skills compared to those of bookish Jesuits.

To be sure, Sahagún was a strange and flighty bird, even for us Franciscans, many of whom are truly "for the birds." He was born and christened Bernadino de Ribera in Spain just seven years after the maiden voyage of Chris Colón. He arrived in present-day Mexico at the age of twenty-two, only eight years after Hernán Cortés ravaged the Aztec capital of Tenochtitlan. At the Colegio Imperial de Santa Cruz de Tlatelolco in 1536, he began to record terms in several Nahuatl dialects in 1536. He then spent the next fifty years of his life compiling a massive archive of twenty-four hundred pages of traditional Aztec knowledge now known as the Florentine Codex.

One section of his archive might be called "talk mesquite to me." It is in the largest of the twelve volumes of his *General History of the Things of New Spain*, which pertains to the natural history of Meso-america seen through the eyes of Nahuatl speakers. I will select just a few terms from this codex recorded by Sahagún. I will also include mesquite terms retained among anonymous Aztec naturalists and artisans. Some were recently elucidated in fascinating detail in a Nahuatl dictionary edited by Frances Karttunen:

1. *mizquicua:* The declarative sentence, "I eat mesquite," rendered shorthand as "I am a mesquite eater."
2. *mizquitl in iatlapal mizquitl, quiltic, memelactic, pipitzahuac, tzatzayanqui, chachayactic:* The leaves of a mesquite tree that are green, straight, slender, serrated, and spreading.

3. *mizquiquiltl:* The edible foliage or *quelites* of mesquite trees.

4. *mizquipahuaci:* The declarative sentence, "I cook mesquite in a pot."

5. *mizquicopalli:* A gum used as a paint or ink derived from a particular kind of mesquite tree.

6. *mizquinechihualeh:* One whose body is adorned with paintings of mesquite symbols.

7. *mizquitequi:* The declarative sentence, "I harvest mesquite wood," rendered shorthand as "I am a mesquite cutter."

8. *mizquiyo:* Mesquite wood cut, owned, or managed by a particular man.

9. *mizquicuahuitl:* A male human torso that was metaphorically so muscular and hard that it was said to be "hewn of mesquite wood."

10. *imizquiyo:* A term referring to the ritual practice of covering the devil's (Uitzilopochtli's) mesquite wood member (a sculpture of a penis?) with a dough made of amaranth seeds and fish puree.

11. *mizquinechihualeh:* Adorned with spiral symbols signifying wind and the curvaceous pods and branches of mesquite.

12. *mizquicuahuitl:* The bark and outer rings of mesquite wood (for burning) that are regarded as being sooty, smoky, and rough to breathe.

13. *mizquitl auh ihuan in cacahuacuahuitl ipan quicueptia mizquitl:* A legendary group of cacao trees that a spirit or deity had transformed into mesquite trees.

14. *Mizquitlah:* A legendary *mezquital* full of wild beasts including the ocelot, the wolf, the bobcat, the serpent, the spider, the rabbit, and the deer, and many herbs.

15. *Quetzalmitzquitl:* The sacred Quetzal bird's own mesquite tree, used as a special roost.

Needless to say, if the mind is the human organ that triggers the most sensory, sensual, and sexual responses, then this vocabulary attests to the fact this tree was writ large in ancient Nahuatl cosmology. But why was it also magnified in the Aztec libido? Did their shaman recognize that this tree had an energy or spirit that few other trees could surpass?

There is a hint of the exceptional powers conferred on mesquite trees in the lore of another Uto-Aztecan culture, the Yaqui or Yoeme of Sonora. They affirm that just two kinds of plants—mesquite and sacred tobacco—have *supernatural* powers over and above the natural powers that most other plants have to nourish and to cure.

But only the mesquite—or *hu'upa* as the Yaquis call it—has the unique power to detect and vanquish witchcraft. That's why the legendary Talking Stick of the Yoemem is carved out of mesquite wood—it informs its people of the presence of both good and evil.

And so, just where does that same tree stand among us today? Is the Talking Tree still speaking to us? Are we even listening? Do we look up to it, or down on it? Has it lost its power over us, or have we forfeited our intimacy with it?

To cut to the chase, do I still have a shot at becoming one with this powerful tree?

CHAPTER THREE

Feeling

"*Do trees have feelings?*" *I asked myself just before I awakened, shaken from a steamy dream, and clumsily fell off the edge of our bed onto the wooden floor.*

"*Ouch,*" *I said.*

"*Ouch yourself,*" *the floor retorted. "That hurt me more than it's gonna hurt you . . ."*

I guess that answers my dreamy question.

Amazingly, my wife, Laurus nobilis, *continues to sleep peacefully, keeping the tree spirits at bay.*

I quietly crawl across the floor and out of the bedroom, into the kitchen, to heat up a pot of tea. There, leaning over the dining room table of iridescent polished mesquite planks, I take my first glimpse of the breaking day. It looks like a good 'un. I look down at my feet, too: It seems that mycorrhizae and nodules on my rootlets are growing longer and more tangled day by day. It seems that my metamorphosis is advancing.

As I add a drizzle of mesquite honey to my tea, I look out through our dining room windows to that world framed by the feathery leaflets or "pinnae" of mesquite trees. It's so pretty—it gives me pinnae envy.

Immediately outside of our straw-bale walls and the suite of windows they support, an arc of slender velvet mesquite trees circumscribes the freshly lit landscape flowing out before me. Their tiny leaflets had folded up at dusk last night, due to the declining intensity of light after sundown, but now they are unfolding before my eyes as the first beams of sunlight break over the mountainous horizon to the east of where I stand.

The trees' sinewy branches reach above me, as if stretching out toward the new day. They ascend far above the windowsills, edge the peripheries of my vision, and descend below the level of the windows.

In early spring, I watch the Hooded orioles arriving from the south, appearing like so many Dreamers taking a tunnel northward into freedom. At the onset of summer, Lazuli buntings appear in bursts of color. They typically select these mesquite boughs for their roosts and perches. Hardly a moment goes by some mornings without some new passerine sitting on its asserine in the mesquite trees just a few feet before me and my cup of tea.

As this particular summer morning begins for me, the sky is as clear as a bell. I can already hear the buzz sawing of the bees on the mesquite blossoms just beyond the window screens. These are Africanized bees.

I watch as a wide-hipped whoop-tailed lizard lumbers up the trunk of a mesquite to bask in the warm afterglow of the dawning sun, as it now reaches like a Border Patrol floodlight over the eastern horizon. The morning has broken, and already there is a flurry of activity to pick up the pieces.

I am a Happy Man this morning, despite a slight bruise on my trunk from falling out of bed. But I am also one who is as inclined as any to look for "the action" and "some satisfaction" in the world around me.

So I sit back and keenly watch the show of creatures, line dancing across the tree's umbrella-like canopy, right before my very eyes. I realize that I am dazzled not merely by mesquite as a solitary tree, but also by mesquite as a full-fledged community of beings.

Then, suddenly, a new realization rises up and bites me on the ash, or in this case, on the mesquite: *After years of dutifully recording all the names of the abundant wildlife I have found to be attracted to mesquite trees, I realize that I may have missed another part of the action*—subtle but significant kinds of action that occur within and upon the mesquites themselves. Until now, I have always focused on what's within the desert forest community, but not on what's found *within the tree.*

What I mean is this: *What's goin' on* with and within the sensibilities and intelligence of each mesquite seedling, sapling, sprawling shrub, or senile but stately tree? What's the life like for the tree itself, not of all the other lives that merely treat it like some Ramada Inn?

Now, by sensibility, I mean a tree's capacity to detect activities and conditions relevant to its survival and reproduction: the current temperature, wind speed, level of humidity, and how they shift with signals from its neighbors, friends, or foes. By intelligence, I mean its capacity to take in that information and make sense of what to do with its life accordingly, changing its stature, its spiny-ness, its reproductive behavior, or its willingness to intertwine its life with those of certain of its neighbors.

The great bio-philosopher Humberto Maturana once put it in this rather geeky manner:

> Living systems are cognitive systems, and living as a process is a process of cognition.
> This statement is valid for all organisms, with or without a nervous system.

Whoa! Did Maturana suggest that *cognition*—perception, insight, discernment—can be accomplished with or without a bit of nervousness on the plant's part? That entire notion has made me a little nervous, so I dipped further into the writings of those who affirm that a plant may be as intelligent as you or me. And what I found is that Maturana and his friend Francisco Varela, since they formulated their Santiago Theory of Cognition in the 1970s, have framed the intelligence of organisms like mesquites in the following manner:

The organization of the living being is a special network system or pattern called *autopoiesis*.

Wait a minute! Are they suggesting that a mesquite is not only intelligent, but may be creative as well? That a plant can be a poet, a painter, a song catcher, or a yarn spinner as long as it has the right materials? Methinks that italicized word *autopoiesis* means something like "self-generating creativity or innovation."

For me, a mesquite truly is poetry in motion, or the choreographer of the desert plant community.

Now, along with this notion that a mesquite is a sensitive, discerning, responsive, and creative being, the tree is considered to be coupled with its habitat in a rather seamless manner. It dynamically responds to its environment chemically, structurally, behaviorally, intelligently, caringly, and intimately, just as lovers do with one another.

No wallflower, that mesquite; it is out on the dance floor doing the boogie! Through recurrent interactions between the tree and its habitat, structural and chemical changes occur in both, but the environment does not really dictate what the tree will be—it only triggers its responses.

It makes the mesquite get up and dance, in a rumble of love. The tree's trajectory reshapes the environment by creating its own sheltering microclimate, its own soil fertility, and its own soundscape.

And that soundscape bursts out into joyous song whenever we join with trees in some kind of erotic dance within the landscape we share.

This is what the great ecologist G. Evelyn Hutchinson called "the ecological theater and the evolutionary play." And this is what a more recent champion of trees' sentience—David George Haskell —means when he says,

> Songs are the sounds that emerge from trees and echo within their wood. Songs are also the stories behind these sounds, telling of life's many interconnections.

Now, this might seem a bit lofty or woo-woo to you at first notice. But recently, two highly regarded scientists—Fritjof Capra and Pier Luigi Luisi—have described the principles by which a multistemmed honey mesquite begins to create its own little sanctuarylike hummock out in the drifting sands of the Chihuahuan Desert, just as an alligator builds its own islandlike nest in the flowing waters of the Everglades:

> Living systems, then, respond to disturbances from the environment autonomously . . . by rearranging their patterns of connectivity. In other words, a living system has the autonomy to decide what to notice and what will disturb it. . . . By specifying which perturbations from the environment trigger changes, *it brings forth a world.*

That's right: *It brings forth a world,* a microcosm with the desert that is in ways less desertlike. It may be a closed-canopy bosque of gigantic honey mesquites growing along the Colorado River floodplain creating its own distinctive habitat with its own microclimate and fauna. Or it may be a hummock on an otherwise pancake-flat desert plain.

That latter process of autopoiesis occurs whenever a multistemmed honey mesquite catches enough sand and silt to grow small-scale hummocks into full-fledged dunes at the *Medanos de Samalayuca* just south of the Rio Grande near El Paso and Juarez.

Pretty good architects and landscape designers, those mesquite trees are, no?

Now, I am not presuming that a mesquite has a heart, mind, or soul just like yours or mine. (You can thank the Creator that mesquite does not have one just like mine, for the tree might sue me for identity theft.) *They don't have to be just like us to be smart!*

Nonetheless, it is fair to say that a mesquite has feelings and pursues *choices* through means very different from those of us who aspire to be *Homo proto-sapiens*, the so-called soon-to-be wisest guys of all sentient beings.

1 so, here comes my big confession, the most massive mea culpa of all plant ecologists' mea culpas ever echoed over the face of this earth: After years of trying to ascertain what this tree means to me and the other creatures around me, I confess that I have largely ignored one now-undeniable fact: *Mesquite trees themselves have feelings and intelligence.*

Feelings. I know, I know . . . it sounds like I'm venturing deep into the woo-woo land of New Age cosmology or wishful teleology to make such an affirmation, however metaphorical it may be. Perhaps someone surreptitiously switched out the mesquite brownie I brought in my lunch pail today for an Alice B. Toklas brownie with psychoactive properties.

Intelligence? Although they have never taken IQ tests (and therefore none of them are known to have flunked them), it has become quite evident that they are far more discerning, say, than the average drunk in a bar five minutes before closing time.

But here's the news, folks: Plant physiologists, ecologists, and evolutionary biologists have already beaten me to the punch in voting for mesquites as sensitive and intelligent beings. *No joke.*

This may come as *new* news to you, but a whole generation of scientists have unabashedly revealed, dutifully documented, and statistically confirmed that mesquite trees are sensitive to touch and that they sense color. They cleanse, protect, and heal their tissues after wounds and infections. Individual trees recognize and respond in different manners to their neighbors, enemies, and allies.

Furthermore, mesquites seek to attract certain allies with their nectar and their sugary pods while repelling certain browsers and borers with their sharp thorns and tough bark. And yet, like most of us, when they fail to escape harm from all of their adversaries, they copiously weep tears to shroud and succor their wounds. This helps them curb the intrusion of further disease and desiccation so that they more quickly and fully recover from their afflictions.

Call it a mesquite medicine bundle for self-healing if you wish. This is not hocus-pocus, not fake news. Mesquite trees can produce a wide array of pharmacologically active salves, pitches, and gums that they can selectively match to the kind of wound from which they are suffering.

Would that I could do that when I feel hurt.

And so, my fellow and fella Mesquiteers, if I am to give you a true and authentic sense of the life of this tree, I must first confess that we will be dealing with the life of a sentient being who "smarts" now and then.

Do not assume that I have put the wrong kind of herb in my teacup this morning. Let me account for the means by which a mesquite tree can sense light, color, heat, wounding, girdling, cutting, or dangerous predators in ways distinctively different from our own.

You see, mesquite trees have gone through a lot over thirty-five millennia in American deserts, including a host of calamities, catastrophes, stresses, depressions, breakups, and near-death experiences.

They've been around the block a few times.

No doubt, these physical, chemical, and social pressures have selectively shaped which trees have survived and reproduced, reinforcing some strategies for survival over others. Some of the survival lessons that they have absorbed may now be deeply encoded within their genetic memory, their DNA, and the very way they move (or stay sessile).

Certain of these strategies developed among their ancestors long before the two most abundant Southwestern trees, velvet mesquite (*Prosopis velutina*) and honey mesquite (*Prosopis glandulosa*), emerged as distinctive species. These strategies are in their roots, their geneology . . . they can be detected in printouts from Ancestry .com. This suggests that such features may be shared not only among the various species of *Prosopis*—their genus or kind—but among more distant relatives in the family of legumes, like acacias, mimosas, and carob trees. Some of these features are more blatantly expressed in some of their kin than in their own little genomes.

But if you scratch the surface of a mesquite tree a little bit, you will find them there as well.

If I've already lost you, let me give you a "fur-instance" from one of their more famous kin. Have you ever lived with a sensitive plant? I did, when I was a kid. I had a potted specimen of *Mimosa pudica* in my bedroom window that I would water daily. After having given it a salutary drink, I would gingerly touch its leaflets to watch them curl up, close inward, and then droop.

At a time in my life when I felt rather shy and distant from my peers, the presence of a sensitive plant that was so unconditionally responsive to me was a salve for my soul. The irony, which escaped me at that time, was that the sensitive plant's Latin species name, *pudica,* suggests that it is "modest, emotionally sensitive, shy, and prone to feeling shame."

Being a relatively clueless guy who may lack the gene for sensitivity myself, it took me a while to notice that leaflets of a mesquite are also responsive to light and touch. Now, the mesquite will never beat out an acacia for the honor of Most Sensitive Plant of the Year, but it is not a passive wallflower either.

The same mechanisms function in both, as a rather shy fellow named Charles Darwin once figured out. His insight came years after he first saw several mesquites and mimosas growing together in the wilds of South America. Charged by that memory about the same time he was suffering from a bad case of dysautonomia, Charles decided to employ his son Francis to undertake several experiments to discern the responsiveness of the leaves of mesquites and other legumes to light, heat, touch, water loss, and gravity. These experiments occurred as the elder Darwin was beginning work on what became one of his lesser-known works, *The Power of Movement in Plants.*

Just imagine how the world might be different today if Darwin had been bold enough to name that book *The Origin of Feeling in Plants.* But the elder Darwin couldn't quite get to such a sweet spot, given that he was a bit distracted by his years of suffering from malaise, muscle spasms, vertigo and vomiting, cramps and colics, headaches and hallucinations, as well as a sensation of impending death and loss of consciousness.

Apparently, such maladies had afflicted him the entire time he had been working on his other little project, a "science fiction fantasy" called *The Origin of Species*. It's a wonder that creationists haven't simply disqualified everything that Darwin ever worked on as the figments of the imagination of a feverishly sick man!

Nevertheless, the younger Darwin was able to discern on his father's behalf that certain kinds of movement among leaflets literally hinge on the *pulvinus,* a group of cells that form a jointlike cluster at the base of mesquite leaves and their leaflets. Pulvini, mind you, are only common in the bean family and among a few members of the "prayer plant" family (a group of herbs with starchy roots that remain staunch creationists to this day).

These pressurized cells collectively function like miniaturized hydraulic pumps to open or close, raise or lower the leaflets or pinnae, which collectively compose the true composite leaf of a mesquite. They make leaflets fold up or open just like Transformer toys!

Now, here's the kinda sexy part (maybe): As the foot-candles of light increase when the sunrise approaches, the leaflets that had gone limp at dusk feel their turgidity surge with excitability! They rise with the dawn to unfold and stretch out in order to take in more sun!

When fully turgid with ample water and loads of revved-up potassium ions, the leaflets stand erect and fully open. (Gasp!) But then when light, touch, or water stress triggers an "electric pulse" or osmotic signal, the many potassium ions suddenly drain away from the pulvinus cells, leaving them flaccid! Their pressure levels drop so low that the outstretched leaves curl up and go to sleep, sort of ruining the whole affair.

It's such a shame: All the leaflets turn in upon themselves, as a means to either avoid further titillation or to buffer themselves from more stress.

But all is not lost! The calcium in these cells suddenly allows them to regulate the outpouring of potassium in a manner that miraculously makes them capable of responding *to touch.*

It may all just sound far too sensuous to believe, but wait a minute—some crafty scientists have found a way to negate all that sensuality just to prove that it truly existed!

A century after the father-and-son team of Darwins first documented the movements of mesquite leaves, two formidable Texas scientists figured out how to make the leaves sit still. The physiologists J. R. Baur and P. W. Morgan did so by applying the herbicide known as picloram to the roots of mesquite seedlings. Imagine that—demonstrating that the very liveliness of a mesquite could be arrested simply by spraying it with a chemical that could potentially kill it!

Just to be fair, Baur and Morgan also applied picloram to the honey mesquite's sidekick in the Chihuahuan Desert, the fragrant acacia known as huisache. Once absorbed by the roots of these seedlings, the picloram stimulated so much production of ethylene in these legumes that their leaves stopped responding to the stimuli of light and touch altogether!

Overwhelmed by ethylene, the mesquite leaflets lost their ability to move out of harm's way. They became sitting ducks! They could no longer escape from excessive heat, damaging sunlight, or physical contact with a human finger.

In essence, the scientists had forced mesquite and huisache to "play dead" rather than being sensitive and responsive. The scientists had mastered the means to make sensitive plants insensitive!

What a strange way to prove that under healthy conditions— free of the influence of herbicides—these plants were indeed sentient beings. Those science guys should win a Nobel Prize for perfecting the art of reductionism!

Notwithstanding this brief lapse into insensitivity, most mesquites and acacias have retained the capacity to form relationships with a group of ants that can protect them. These trees literally have ants in their pants . . . or ants in their spines, crotches, and canopies. The ants help boat-spined acacias and mesquites evade damage by herbivorous browsers like cud-chewing cattle and headlight-dazed deer, or even by human woodcutters.

In the bizarre case of boat-spined acacias, *Pseudomyrmex ferruginea* ants offer the plants a defense against undue competition from other plants.

Whoa, think about that one for a moment. The acacias supply the ants with a veritable keg of sugar-rich nectar in exchange for the ants serving as "bouncers" to repel anyone who tries to crash the party!

Like these acacias, some mesquites produce copious amounts of nectar in glands just below their flowers, which of course are the more typical factories of nectar production in most legume trees. These "extra-floral nectaries" then attract a group of marauding twig ants that nest in dead branches and trunk scars of both mesquite and acacia trees.

Around where I live, two kinds of twig ants serve as bodyguards for velvet mesquites: *Pseudomyrmex apache* and *P. pallidus*. While not exclusively found on mesquites, as *P. ferruginea* ants are on boat-spined acacias, these other twig ants can also serve as bad-ass bouncers for any troublemakers who enter the mesquite bosque.

It has even been claimed by ecologist Tim Flannery that "the saliva of leaf-eating insects can be 'tasted' by the leaf being eaten. In response, the tree sends out a chemical signal that attracts predators [like ants] that feed on that particular leaf-eating insect."

Whoa! Whoa! Whoa! Wait a minute! A leaflet samples a bit of saliva and discerns by "taste" whether it was spit up by a friend or a foe? Does that mean the plant is a carnivore?

Curiously, when such defender ants sense that their host is about to be attacked, they go on a shit-kicking rampage. We are not exactly sure which distress chemical or pheromone pulls the trigger that shoots mesquite twig ants into a raging frenzy.

Perhaps the ants read these warning signals from the tree as it reduces its nectar production or sends out a sharp chemical alarm to announce that something is aggravating the hell out of it!

When the ants get the message, they become so ferocious that they are apt to go into a stinging spree against any intruders, including middle-aged Bubbas wielding mighty chainsaws and massive pruning shears. They are like little Davids up against Goliaths, for a single Bubba may weigh as much as the combined weight of 90 million ants.

Most commonly, the ants go after horses, cows, deer, and prong-horn antelope coming in to browse the foliage or consume the pods of mesquites.

Nevertheless, I have heard of at least two instances where mesquite twig ants swarmed and bit mesquite woodcutters so many times that they had to flee and be treated for the stings.

MESQUITE

My old friend Justin Schmidt has ranked *Pseudomyrmex* stings at 1.8 on a scale of 4 in his Schmidt Hymenopteran Sting Pain Index, comparing it to "having someone fire a staple into your cheek."

Oh, that Justin, he'll do anything for fun. He has voluntarily submitted himself to being stung by more than 150 kinds of venomous hymenopterans, including *Pseudomyrmex* ants. Like some sommelier in a tasting room for fine wines, Justin describes the effects of the boat-spined acacia twig ant as "a rare, piercing, elevated sort of pain . . ."

Oh well. For now, you might want to stick with a sting from a mesquite twig ant that is more "of medium body, with a little hint of bitterness" like a Cabernet Franc from Hungary, or a sweeter sting that is more "stimulating, with grip and tension, powerful but full of finesse," like a Moelleux wine from France.

Remarkably, *Pseudomyrmex* twig ant species like *P. ferruginea* have been known to cut the competing branches of other trees threatening to shade out or dry up the sweet nectar provided by their sponsoring legume tree. They thereby ensure that their boat-spined acacia host plant is not deprived of the resources of solar radiation, soil, and water that are needed to feed and harbor the ant colony itself.

Now *that* is pretty damned smart for an ant with a brain that is only 1/40,000th the size of the average human noggin.

Of course, mesquites and acacias have other ways to defend themselves from intruders. Among their best means of defense are the substantial thorns that arm their branches and deter breakage and browsing by bulls, cows, stags, and does.

Once the trees reach a certain size and girth and cannot be as easily damaged, the average length of their thorns diminishes. But it appears that when their branches have been significantly damaged by cattle or wildlife, some mesquite saplings grow longer thorns with devastating puncture power and a painful toxin on their tips.

My CowHippy friend, rancher Dennis Moroney, pays homage to the mesquite thorns that make his life difficult on the 47 Ranch just north of Bisbee, Arizona:

Mesquite is not merely difficult to eradicate; it exacts revenge. When you hack it back with an ax, it will reassert itself in a revenge-seeking cycle by sending out a rash of new thorns that are needle-sharp and meant to kill or maim. It produces a dozen resprouts for every trunk you cut, and the new thorns on them are three to four times longer than the original ones. I figure that some weeks on our ranch, we put in at least ten hours just repairing and plugging tires after mesquite thorns have punctured them.

Another old friend of mine, desert ecologist Martin Karpiscak, once admitted to me how discouraging and difficult it had been for him to study thorniness. He tried to scientifically determine whether certain genetic strains of mesquite respond more than others to the perils of the desert world with a penchant for thorniness. Martin had tried experimentally inducing defensive armature in mesquites found on rangelands being actively grazed by cattle, but had no luck.

Perhaps the reason that Martin could not solve this thorny problem was that mesquite's responses are in some ways still shaped less by cattle and more by some "ghosts of evolution" that once lived intimately with this tree. These ghosts will reappear elsewhere in this book, for mesquite has surrounded itself with bansheelike evolutionary anachronisms. That's right: *anachronisms,* i.e., old and obsolete, just like me and perhaps some of you, dear readers.

When mesquites do get wounded, whipped, infected, or otherwise stressed by wind, heat, drought, or girdling insects, they have demonstrated a rather astonishing capacity for self-healing. *Presto!* Once they recognize that they are substantially injured, they exude either a black sticky pitch or a pale brown salvelike gum that leaks antimicrobial compounds onto the surface of their wounds in order to fend off fungal and bacterial infections that can cause decay or even death to tree tissues.

The most effusive weeping of mesquite gums seems to come on particularly stressful days when air temperatures exceed 95 degrees Farenheit, when dry winds are fierce, and when sucking or girdling insects are particularly voracious.

I myself weep a lot on days when the temperatures around my home exceed 95 degrees Farenheit, when dry winds are fierce, and when sucking or girdling insects are particularly ruthless in their attacks on me. I call such crying spells "bad mesquite days."

But I have recently learned that the riddle of who or what actually triggers the profuse weeping of mesquite gums is far more complex than I have ever imagined on my own. Juan Orozco Villafuerte, a brilliant young chemical ecologist in Mexico, found that there was more to how wounded mesquites heal than what meets the (tearful) eye.

Juan found that mesquites weep more gum from wounds in their branches and trunks. This is particularly true when insects that suck into the sap of a stressed-out mesquite carry certain kinds of fungi and bacteria in their mouths.

I get infected gums, too. And that's why I gargle.

But wait! There's more!

Juan found that these microbes—a powdery fungus named *Aspergillus nidulans*—and a strange proteobacterium found in dirt and swimming pools—*Pseudomonas pseudoalcaligenes*—could "elicit" or "stimulate" the weeping of mesquite gums. They *catalyze* a more intense flow of gums, for crying out loud.

And so, a mesquite tree injured by a Husqvarna ax or a Brahman bull horn or a Caterpillar tractor is exposed to higher doses of the peculiar chemicals produced by the wood-rotting microbes. The tree begins to weep more gum to cover its wounds, thereby reducing the long-term damage from such attacks.

Do you get it? It's actually the chemical ecology of these bacteria and fungi in the mouthparts of insects—*not the wood-rotting insects themselves*—that makes this magic work. The chemical arsenal in the microbes triggers the flow of mesquite gums out of the tree, and these "exudates" are like liquid bandages, sealing off the wounds of bull-battered, ax-cut, or wind-whipped branches.

That's right: The microbes are in charge of the process, just like they are in the "magic" of love. Do you know what I mean? It's like the microbes that you carry in your sweat that either make you stink to high heaven or make your potential partner swoon.

Do you know what I'm talking about—the scientific discovery of the century? If you haven't yet heard, I hate to break the news to you, but it's not your genome and your perspiration that your partner is attracted to, it's the fragrance of the microbes you haul around in your pits!

Word of this discovery has apparently been widely and *wildly* disseminated, for I recently overheard the following conversation in the men's locker room of a gym I frequent.

"I don't know what to do, buddy; my girlfriend just told me that she's sure she doesn't love me, but she really loves the fragrance of the microbes in my sweat. I mean, like, what's a dude to do? *She's left me for some bacterium that formerly lived in the pits of my sweatshirt!*"

"Like, don't overthink it, bro'; you're playing mind games with yourself. Just be sure to sweat a lot more whenever you're around her . . ."

Now, I know I've been straying a bit from the theme of arboreal love, but let's take all of this book-larnin' back into the mesquite canopy and the bosque woodland that forms when two or more mesquites come together in holy ma-*tree*-mony. It is there that certain insects (and their microbes) serve as beauticians, chaperones, cosmetologists, matchmakers, makeover artists, and dating coaches for a tree and its potential mates.

Just for starters, when longhorn beetles girdle, trim, and shape mesquite branches, the trees change their architecture and their reproductive capacity accordingly. The more the tree is stressed by drought, the less likely it is that the girdled branches will ever resprout from the stubs left after the longhorn beetles have girdled them so that they can more easily deposit their insect eggs in the mesquite tree's cambium.

The pruned-back, stressed-out trees will ultimately flower and fruit less frequently than better-watered trees. Their checking account has been so depleted that their blossoms bounce!

In contrast, the branches of mesquite trees in wetter habitats will have a greater capacity to resprout. Their branches will grow to greater heights, so that their flowers and edible pods will be positioned well beyond the reach of small herbivores, allowing more seeds to be dispersed to safe sites for germination and survival.

Who would have thunk it? Mesquite's interactions with organisms we hardly notice—girdling longhorn beetles and the fungi and bacteria in the beetles' mouths—could change the overall shape, survivability, longevity, and reproductive capacity of a humble tree. And if they can do that, can't they also change the destiny of the human stewards who depend upon mesquite for food, fiber, fuel, and frolic?

But it is not just the pale brown or amber tears of mesquite gums that can heal and change the course of desert history. The black tar-like pitch of mesquite is also pretty potent. It is called *flux*.

One desert dweller I know once complained to me that when he parked his favorite Corvette under a mesquite tree, it dripped a gummy pitch onto the hood, stripping off the painted finish.

His car looked horrible. No self-respecting female of *any* species would go out with him. After a while, he conceded that he should sell his car and his other possessions and become a celibate hermit out in a cave in the most remote stretches of the Snorin' Desert.

There he reached spiritual enlightenment, which apparently ranked higher (in his mind) on Justin Schmidt's Sting Pain Index than dates in Corvettes. See how potent mesquite gum can be?

Not surprisingly, most indigenous desert dwellers apparently knew this before it appeared in the pages of *Plant Physiology and Biochemistry* or *Population Ecology*. Over the centuries, they have found mesquite saps, gums, and pitches to be effective medicines for curing a variety of maladies.

These mesquite exudates were used to cure eye ailments by everyone from the Aztecs living in Central Mexico to the Apaches living above and below the Mogollon Rim of the US Southwest. The black gum was dissolved in hot water, and the dark liquid that resulted was used as eye drops, eyewashes, and lotions. Healers from at least a dozen native nations offered these remedies to those of their people who had lost their vision.

But mesquite gums and pitches were also widely used to purge native people's gastrointestinal systems of toxins, irritants, and blockages.

The black pitch can also be mixed with mesquite leaves to brew a tea, which could then be drunk as an emetic until the problem was resolved.

The antimicrobial power of such teas has also been found to reduce the pain and persistence of sore throats, deep throats, and horse throats. The teas could also cure upset stomachs, indigestion, constipation or diarrhea, dyspepsia, and leather.

It is quite possible that desert dwellers first learned how to use mesquite gums for their digestive problems by watching other mammals self-medicate. I once sat beneath a mesquite tree watching a sphinx moth self-medicate on the hallucinogenic nectar of jimsonweed, which was far more fun than watching hippies self-medicate in the mud at Woodstock when I was a teenager.

If that is not enough to convince you to sequester some mesquite gum in your medicine cabinet, maybe you'll also want to keep some around for healing your chapped laps, the cracked or cut skin of your fingers and toes, sensitive tissues bruised or broken by childbirth, or your fallen fontanel . . .

I don't want to sound messianic about all of this. I just want to suggest to you that mesquite has feelings, and those feelings sometimes surge into healing powers.

Why might that be true? Because mesquite has suffered from many of the same wounds, toxins, and maladies that you or I might suffer from over our lifetimes, during our own desert sojourns and residencies here on earth. Perhaps it is no wonder that what it does to heal itself might also serve to help the rest of us who live in its midst.

As I finish my tea of fresh green mesquite leaves sweetened with the honey made by the bees that dwell here with us on this rocky ridge in Patabutta, Arizona, I insert a tiny droplet of gummy mesquite sap in to my mouth and chew upon it as a digestive. It makes me salivate, like all good lovers do.

MESQUITE

I guess it's time for me to go into the kitchen to prepare some mesquite flour waffles for my wife, who has now awakened to the buzzing of the bees outside of our window. I'm still wondering whether she has fully realized how much I've fallen for mesquite.

CHAPTER FOUR

Nectar

Now, bear with me, as I digress from arboreality for a moment.

When I was little, one way I figured out just who I was gonna be when I grew up was by watching the kinds of characters that could be my potential role models. I was initially attracted to colorful down-and-outers who "walked on the wild side": rock musicians, farmers, chefs, bartenders, bootleggers, presiding officers of Dead Poets Societies, beaten prizefighters, political leaders who had fallen out of favor, roust-abouts, and rounders of every color and caliber.

Later, when I realized how close I was to becoming a mesquite, I began to take notice of all the characters who hung out with these trees in the bosque beyond our neighborhood's edge. It was time to pay attention not just to mesquites themselves, but to all the other kinds of neighbors, friends, adversaries, and allies in a mesquite community that I might be opening my life to.

What did they eat when they got together? What was their favorite music? How allegiant were they to one another? These questions, it seemed to me, should be issues of critical concern to anyone on the verge of changing their identity, their location, their vocation, and their avocation. Personal transformations may confer certain benefits, but they may also come at a hefty price.

MESQUITE

Now, I am no gossip, but there always seemed to be a buzz about what was going on at the mesquite bosque down at the end of our street on Redrock Creek, just past the edge of Patabutta village.

When springtime sails into the desert borderlands, you would not be wrong if you guessed that you would soon be hearing love songs in the air. As you walk through the groves of mesquite growing along Redrock Creek, or any other intermittent watercourse, it seems that the world is abuzz with bees busy visiting the sweet scent of flowers. The Summer of Love appears to be just around the corner.

Now, don't think I'm sappy enough to suggest that you'll be hearing Rimsky-Korsakov's hackneyed old classic, *The Flight of the Bumblebee.* Nope. That's lightweight compared to the sounds coming out of a full-fledged orchestra that includes no less than five dozen distinctive bee species playing in any mesquite patch. They are doing their part in a symphonic rendition of *The Dance of the Desert Bees,* a masterpiece that includes one thousand to twelve hundred distinct species of pollinators found between the Silverbell Hills in Ironwood Forest National Monument, northwest of us in the Sonoran Desert, and San Bernardino National Wildlife Refuge, southeast of us on the edge of the Chihuahuan Desert.

That's a lot of musicians packed into the same orchestra pit! They include sixty-four kinds of bees found buzzing around mesquite flowers by Jeff Neff in Ironwood, and ninety-six identified by Bob Minckley in and around the San Bernardino refuge. Within a hundred-fifty-mile arc of these mesquite-dominated landscapes you can find what my buddy Stephen Buchmann calls "the richest bee real estate anywhere in the world," harboring nearly a fourth of all native bees in North America.

Sure enough, you can hear the ubiquitous buzz of the introduced honeybee and the vibrating hum of huge carpenter and cactus bees, the tubas and bassoons of this symphony orchestra. But most of the music is coming from the piccolos and clarinets, the flutes and pennywhistles of the desert symphony: diggers and sweat bees, leafcutters and mason bees, tarantula hawk wasps and hoverflies.

They come in all shapes and sizes, textures and colors, striped and solid. Some are ground nesters while others plug their eggs into the twigs and hollow stems of grasses, herbs, and shrubs. Only a few are brooded communally, in dense colonies; most are as solitary as a monk on a mountain top.

And their names? Their names are as diverse as those of the member countries of the United Nations: *Agapostemon* and *Ashmeadiella; Chalicodoma* and *Colletes; Diadasia* and *Dolichostelis; Megachile* and *Nomia; Pepsis* and *Perdita; Xeromelecta* and *Zacosmia!*

Some of these illustrious pollinators are specialists on just a few related forms of blooms, while others fly and forage around the 'hood, visiting any blossom that will let them in. But there are also true mutualists of the mesquite, which hardly pay any other kind of flower any mind at all.

Their vernacular names give them away: *Ashmeadiella prosopidis,* the mesquite-loving leafcutter bee; and *Colletes prosopidis,* the mesquite-loving plasterer or polyester bee, who apparently wears polyester pantsuits on occasion; and several *Perdita* species, the tiny sand-mining bees that get "lost" in the canopies of giant mesquite trees.

Just what are they all after? Well, it may not look like there is much nectar and pollen in each perfect little flower on a mesquite, but a single tree can produce more than a million and a half flowers per season.

Count 'em up: Each diminutive flower or "floret" might contain as many as thirty pollen grains, but some produce nectar while others are nectarless. Each flowering spike on a mesquite branch can produce more than 250 florets, and an average mesquite tree of some size might produce five to six thousand spikes over the course of a spring and a summer.

I realize that you may not have this statistic right at your fingertips, but the yield of bee food per tree might be as high as 72,000 milligrams or 2.5 ounces of nectar per tree, and 5 ounces of pollen grains per tree. At 200 mature velvet mesquite trees per acre, that's more than 30 pints of nectar per acre, or more than 6 pounds of pollen per acre patch of mesquite habitat.

That may not initially look like much to write home to your momma about, but think again: Those quantities can provide the bulk of the nourishment needed by many bees living out their lives under arid conditions. What's more, the bloom and the pollen production of mesquite trees hardly ever fails. I reckon that whether rain or snow or sleet or drought come to ravish the desert, at least some mesquites make it through to flower and fruit, a constancy that most of their pollinators or seed dispersers appreciate.

So what if I am a solitary bee and nearly all my food and drink come from the nectar and pollen of desert mesquite trees, year in and year out? What if nearly all the stable isotopes in a bee's cells can be traced back to a particular "resource island" of mesquites? What if that bee spends nearly all of its foraging time on and under the canopy of a mesquite that serves as a nurse plant for its other food sources as well?

For all intents and purposes, doesn't the identity of the bee overlap with the identity of its nurse tree—mesquite—even though they have different genetic origins? Could we make the claim that the many bees swarming around a mesquite are like the rings circling around Saturn, which are so strongly associated with that planet that they are essentially one and the same? Or may we regard those bees that depend upon a mesquite tree (which in turn depends upon them for regeneration) in much the same way that we regard the myriad microbes in your own eyes, nose, and throat, as if they are part and parcel of one body, *your body?*

All I am saying is that it is terribly hard for me to determine where the arboreality of a mesquite tree ends and the distinctive being of these bees begins.

And I suppose I could make the same claim about most lovers. . . . and some codependents as well.

But there is another kind of fuzzy set that I imagine when I ponder bees on mesquite trees in the Sonoran Desert. It is actually hard to separate out the influence of mesquites on the sum total of life in the Sonoran Desert as a whole. Of course, desert ecologists have surely tried to do so. Their dandy mathematical exercises like principal components analysis might move us toward some distinctions, but they still can't get us very far.

Let me give you a rather sweet example of what I mean. Many beekeepers in Sonora and Arizona label their value-added products as *mesquite honey*. That is a fair description of what may be in their jars and squeeze bottles, because their top-bar hives may have been placed in the shade of a mesquite tree or seasonally moved around an entire grove of these trees.

But what any honest beekeeper in southern Arizona or Sonora will concede is that mesquite honey is really shorthand for Sonoran Desert honey, revealing a blend of influences from mesquites, ironwoods, acacias, creosote bushes, hackberries, and a dozen-some seasonal wildflowers. Sometimes it is a pale, almost creamy amber; other times it is a somewhat darker, stickier syrup. As you close your eyes and plop a spoonful of desert honey onto your tongue, you begin to savor wave after wave of fragrances and flavors wrapped into the delicate, almost smoky, citruslike sweetness we associate with the word *mesquite.*

But what, in fact, we are sampling is a *desert terroir*—a taste of place—shaped by many influences—soil, plant, animal, and fungal —distilled down by harsh weather and centrifuged by gentle human hands.

What we end up with is the essence of a desert existence epitomized by a mesquite tree's engagement with its neighbors in strategies that allow for their collective survival and its rather generous manner of offering nourishment and pleasure to the many other lives intertwined with its own.

It is hard for me to imagine this desert place without the palpable presence of the fragrances and flavors of mesquite blossoms, wood, and sap embedded in it. They are, at the very least, nested sets. And perhaps they are something more intimate than that: nestled sets.

Once I realized how much my own sense of place is related to my sense of taste, it began to change the way I regarded nearly every sweet mesquite I encountered. It changed my senses of allegiance, affinity, and membership as well, just as it may change yours. And that is why I am asking you to raise one hand into the air, put the other one across your heart, and proclaim with me:

> *We pledge allegiance to this flagship species*
> *of the United Desert States of the Americas,*
> *and to the mycorrhizal mass on which it stands,*
> *one cohesive nation in all of creation,*
> *its flora and fauna indivisible,*
> *with love fests and wild times for all.*

Onward, Mesquiteers! I hope you are beginning to realize that when you fall in love with a mesquite, you're not just marrying a single tree, you're being adopted into an entire clan of fungi, bacteria, yeast, understory plants, insects, reptiles, birds, and mammals that go with the tree. You are now in "a family way." It's about mutual support!

No more sleeping alone! The rest of the family always seems to be right there, sleeping and waking, wailing and laughing along with you.

CHAPTER FIVE

Intimacy

Well, now that we find ourselves in a family way, I must also tell you that the honeymoon is over.

I can't tell you how much I was stunned when I found out that mesquite had already had other lovers! Mesquite was already involved in some intimate relationships—in some ménage-a-tree—*with some-bodies other than me! My rude awakening came when I found them cohabiting, in a rather compromising position, cuddling together on the desert floor.*

I guess I should have taken heed of the little hints, the nonverbal signals that could have clued me in to their clandestine relationships, had I been paying sufficient attention. But no, even though the signs were there, I ignored or at least dismissed them, refusing to acknowledge that something was going on behind my back. If I had just gotten up earlier in the morning, I would have spotted that gorgeous bird in a silk nightie, flapping her bicolored wings while moving between the trees, engaging not only with mesquite, but also with the mistletoes hiding within its canopies.

Apparently, Mesquite had been having an affair with Mistletoe and Phainopepla for some time, given the mischievous nicknames they had been using for one another. Phainopepla—that silky flycatcher whose name means "glimmering robe"—was playfully teased as being "mesquite's owner," "mesquite's handler," or "mesquite's tender," depending on who you talk to. In the ancient Pima language, those sentiments are embedded in the name *kuigam,* "mesquite's people." Mistletoe, in Old English, was originally *mistel-tan,* which means "dung on a twig." I know, at first glance, that's not exactly an amorous name, even though the Druids did somehow associate mistletoe with the enhancement of human fertility. And mesquite itself has been nicknamed "thorny dude," "sturdy hunk (of wood)," or "sweet pod," depending upon who you listen to on the streets.

To make sense of the peculiar intimacy shared by the three of them, I had to first get acquainted with the behavior of the flighty member of this affair, phainopepla. I love seeing this bird out at dawn in the ancient forests of tall cacti, ironwoods, and mesquite, moving tree to tree to roost and feed. Phainopepla flits and flirts around a lot, mimicking a dozen other birds' songs and getting into lots of mischief.

When its forays and frolics are done, it seems to love roosting in the highest reaches of mesquite branches, preferring them to those of ironwoods, palo verdes, or acacias in the same neighborhood. Nevertheless, this enigmatic desert presence can be found roosting in all four of these desert legume trees, moving among them at will. Let me just leave it at this: Phainopeplas do not sleep with just one tree.

Of course, this bird is not up there merely to be embraced by the limbs nor to partake of the sweet pods of its favorite tree. It is there to gorge itself on the sticky-sweet, juicy, drupaceous fruit of mesquite's intermingled partner, mistletoe. You can smell the sweet perfume of the flowers and berrylike fruits of mistletoe from yards away.

But mistletoe, too, has its indiscretions, being found with ironwood, palo verde, and acacia, as well as with mesquite, its main squeeze.

As a matter of fact, the more mistletoe is present in a mesquite, the more phainopeplas come around to eat the mistletoe fruit and to defecate its seeds out onto the twigs and limbs of the mesquite (hence the love handle "dung on a twig").

Ecologists call this phenomenon a *positive feedback loop.* The rest of us just recognize it for what it is to the bird at hand: a favorite place to dump one's load.

I don't want you to be distracted by this digression about defecation; I just want to get it out of the way. For what's important here is how mistletoe seeds get stuck on mesquite in a manner that joins the two plants into a seamless union. To be blunt about it, they are doing more than just cuddling together; mistletoe and mesquite, shall we say, are deeply entwined.

In fact, we might claim that mistletoe is stuck on mesquite, literally and figuratively.

You see, mistletoe's berrylike drupes contain seeds that are coated with one of the world's most remarkable bio-adhesives, viscin, which some observers liken to a lovemaking lubricant, while others compare it to an entangling superglue.

Viscin is, as you would expect it to be, viscous. It's a resinous mucopolysaccharide, a polymer of xylose that is highly branched, insoluble, and hard to wash off any surface to which it sticks. It comprises long, thin cellulose microfibers that undergird its elastic, adherent structure. Curiously, phainopepla has a gizzard that shucks the nonadhesive skins off the "berries" of mistletoe, so that the gelatinous goo of microfibers surrounding the seeds can glom onto to anything with which it makes contact.

When fully exposed to moisture, these microthin microfibers don't get washed out and separated from one another. Instead, they get rather slippery and stretch to be hundreds of times longer than they were in their dry, resting state, where they were curled up like a frightened porcupine.

But pass them through a bird's gut, vomit them up out of a bird's beak, or wipe them off the same bird's slobbery bill, and they have enough moist tensile strength to adhere to the top, sides, or bottom of any mesquite branch that comes between them and the desert floor.

I hate to be indelicate, but mistletoe seeds especially like sticking in bark crevices, elbows, armpits, and other "crotches"—that is, crotches of tree trunks where two branches diverge on roads not taken. There, stuck on the dark, moist, rough-barked limbs and in the moist indentations and protrusions of mesquite, the seeds have ample opportunity to germinate. Mistletoe seedlings then find a way to penetrate into mesquite's flesh.

That's right. Mistletoe does not simply grow *onto* the mesquite, as Spanish moss pins itself to an oak trunk and lives there ever after as an epiphyte. Nor does it start at the bottom of the trunk and climb up, as vines do. As Peter Wohlleben suggests,

> Mistletoes save themselves the arduous task of climbing up trees. They prefer to start at the top. . . . Now, way up in those lofty heights, there's water and food aplenty—in the trees. To get at them, the mistletoes sink their roots into the branches they're sitting on and simply suck out what they need.

In fact, their probing root tips do more than that by invading the very plumbing of a mesquite. Their root tissues insinuate themselves into the tree's tissues to sequester water, nitrogen, and micronutrients for their own reproductive success. Mistletoe is both an epiphyte and an endophyte, if you get the drift of where this story is going.

Now, to back up a little: What underscores the ancient intimacy shared between mistletoe's seeds and phainopepla's gut is the rapidity by which the former is passed through the latter. Just like the glorious stickiness of mistletoe berries shucked of their skins, this, too, is an indicator of coadaptation.

For the phainopepla, this adaptation is one that avian ecologists euphemistically call "avian digestive tract transit time." In plain English that means "the pace from drupe to bird poop."

The ecological question is this: *How fast can a bird deliver its droppings after it has eaten some berries?*

For phainopepla, with a gastrointestinal tract about 6 inches long, a bunch of mistletoe seeds can make it down the chute undamaged in less than thirty minutes so that they remain germinable. Under the best circumstances, phainopepla "through-put" can be achieved in as little as eighteen minutes, leaving the mistletoe seeds warm, wet, and ready for sprouting in a crotch, in a knothole, or on the limb of their choice.

Now, I have never personally accumulated much data on issues such as this, but from what ornithologists say, phainopepla is a real Fast Chuter, a veritable Quick Draw compared to most other desert birds, which seem constipated by comparison.

But enough of such crap! What's important to know is that after mistletoe seeds germinate in the tree's crotch or in the many folds, crevices, scars, and depressions of its limbs, the rootlets from seedlings penetrate into the very cambium of the mesquite and then invade the conductive tissues of both the xylem and phloem.

Inside, mistletoe cells essentially become hackers. They form what plant anatomists call *haustoria*, parasitic structures that allow mistletoe to plumb moisture, energy, and nutrients from mesquite's photosynthetic bank account into their own. As my friend Carlos Martinez del Rio, renowned ecologist of mistletoe, has bluntly explained to me: "They really suck plants dry because they evaporate like crazy."

Their big fleshy leaves annually transpire tons of water out of all the mistletoe masses infesting a patch of mesquite trees, leaving their hosts either higher and drier or dead and gone.

Yes, my friends, you can begin to see the picture. Phainopepla and mistletoe have a mutualistic relationship from which both benefit. Phainopepla also benefits from its relationship with mesquite as its roost. But however cuddly it may look, mistletoe is a parasite plaguing mesquite. Not only that, but phainopepla is, in so many words, a disease vector or bearer of bad omens for the mesquite.

Any mistletoe that becomes firmly established in mesquite's canopy ends up competing with its host tree for sunlight and moisture. It also "breaks and enters" to rob the mesquite of its hard-won moisture and energy.

Witches' broom growths of mistletoe can become so heavy that they weigh down and burden the branches of desert trees, eventually breaking them or toppling the entire tree. They seem to preferentially infest mesquites already under stress, due to drops in aquifer levels that have drained moisture away from their mass of roots.

And yet, mesquite is not a passive victim of the liaison between phainopepla and mistletoe. In ways that we do not fully understand, mesquite either physically or chemically resists invasion by mistletoe. Although more mistletoe seeds rain down on mesquite branches from the phainopepla roosts in the highest boughs, mesquite patches in the ancient forests of the Sonoran Desert often have far lower levels of mistletoe invasion and establishment than ironwood, acacia, or palo verde do. It resists being taken advantage of and fully overwhelmed by the other two species in this desert triad.

It has taken me a while to come to grips emotionally with all of this. But now that I have, I feel it might be hard to ever convince me that all three partners can ever have their needs equally satisfied. It just seems inevitable that one partner will come up short and become broken-hearted by all of this illicit commingling.

As a nineteenth-century cowboy song once stated in rather irascible and sexist manner, "One wife on a cow ranch is a-plenty for me." So let me try to update that message in a manner that might be a bit more politically correct:

How do I discern whether one partner in a mesquite patch is a-plenty for me?

CHAPTER SIX

Deep-State

As I have begun to fathom what being a mesquite entails, a rather odd analogy has come to mind:

Mesquite is like a mermaid, in the sense that we seem to be familiar with its upper half, but we are most intrigued if not dumbfounded by its lower half, which is usually kept out of sight, even though it may be where mysteries are most alive.

At first glance, mesquite trees don't really seem all that mysterious. Perhaps that's because many of us categorically dismiss them as being rather short, squat, and disheveled compared to other arboreals we have known. We treat them as humble shrubs—woody wallflowers— not as trees.

I will always remember the complaint of a rather brilliant student from the Yale School of Forestry when she first came face to face with a "stunted" mesquite tree. She had bravely ventured out for a summer of studying the ancient desert forests of mesquites, ironwoods, and colum- nar cacti that grew along the Sonoran coast of the Gulf of California. Then a certain disappointment must have overwhelmed her.

"Well, this desert is surely beautiful, but I'm not so sure that it would it would even qualify as a forest with most of my colleagues back East. . . . I'm not trying to put them down, but the mesquites here are so tiny and widely dispersed that they hardly form a sparse thicket, let alone anything that could be called a forest of contiguous trees."

I must admit, I felt a pang of low self-esteem for a moment, perhaps because I was overidentifying with shrubby mesquites and their scrubby neighbors. I had to concede that my companion's observations were indeed valid—that is, if we only examined the aboveground structure of mesquite patches.

And so, I must ask you all to get up out of your armchairs and stand on your heads. For if we stood on our heads and wore x-ray glasses *to look up into* the rhizosphere of the *mesquital,* we should clearly see above us a dense and towering forest of elongated taproots and tangled banks of rootlets covered with knotty nodules of nitrogen-fixing bacteria and delicate threadlike hyphae. These hyphae form miles of *extra-radical* mycelium bestowed upon three-quarters of all desert plants by the *genius loci* of vascular-arbuscular endomycorrhizal fungi.

How's that for a mouthful of mesquite allies, the ones who truly run the Deep-State?

Now, let's get down to brass *taxis: Taxis* is a rather radical concept meaning "the movement of an organism in response to a stimulus such as light or the presence of food." Based on mesquite trees that have had their root biomass carefully excavated and weighed, there is four or five times more *mobile, stimulated biomass* of a mesquite tree underground than there is aboveground!

Let's put that much underground sentience into perspective: *A four- to five-fold root-to-shoot ratio for a desert mesquite grove is greater than that of any known temperate forest type.* Perhaps it is surpassed only by the root-to-shoot ratios recorded among low-lying shrubs in the arctic tundra, where most of life remains both underground and under ice or snow.

If it helps you to picture the heights and depths of a mesquite in lengths rather than as the weights of its aboveground and belowground biomass, let's picture some of the lankiest mesquite trees known to humankind. Not far from where I live in Santa Cruz County, Arizona, an old hero of mine named Gilbert Sykes once found *the* mesquite in the entire universe most deserving of being placed on the list of American Forests Champion Trees.

This particular mesquite was conferred arboreal sainthood in 1949. This saintly tree was a stately mesquite that stood 46 feet high, with a sinewy torso of 196 inches in circumference, wearing a crown that spread out 60 feet across the desert floor. It is no small feat to get that large in a place renowned for its paucity of humidity and fertility.

But not far from where Gilbert's lofty mesquite gained *national* stature, there grew another one, one that garnered *global* acclaim for the depth of its roots. It too happened to be a velvet mesquite, but one that exhibited such profundity that it outdistanced any other tree known to anchor itself in this earthen planet.

The said mesquite was confirmed to wield a taproot that was found edging the vertical mine shaft of an Arizona copper mine at a depth of more than 175 feet, with a few of its probable rootlets caught reaching down to a 200-foot depth! That is a depth four times the height of the tallest known velvet mesquite! This is a distinction worthy of being immortalized in the annals of *Rootly's Believe It or Not!*

What's more, it hints at the possibility that a truly unexplored forest realm of the grandest proportions may be growing below my own desert home! Who needs to fly to the moon when we have yet to explore the mesquite roots beneath our feet?

Such a revelation prompts those of us who claim to be desert rats to invite our colleagues from the more modest and homely groves of hickories, beeches, and maples to visit our monumental mesquite forests. Once here, we urge them to stand on their heads so that they may glance up with awe at the subterranean kingdom of the Sonoran Desert, perhaps the deepest state of being on our continent. Those who live in regions that suffer from a scarcity of aridity are finally receiving their *comeuppance* and *just deserts*.

Now, just as the mermaid wiggles her fins to navigate the deep sea, so do mesquite trees wiggle their roots to navigate through the depths of dry earth, where they reach a great abundance of hidden moisture teeming below us with considerable verve. Yes, mesquites do have taproots that can tap into ancient aquifers, but they also dazzle their neighbors with shallow lateral roots that snake their way along close to ground level, capturing any bit of moisture spilled from a brief summer rain. And when there is a drought, they can quickly slough off their rootlets as the soil around them begins to get as dry as the bones in a Georgia O'Keefe painting.

It may sound counterintuitive, but drought actually stimulates the growth of mesquite's thicker taproots so that they can extend downward in search of moisture. Necessity *is* the mother of invention. Now, "in search of moisture" may sound a bit too teleological to some of you, but how else would you describe a taproot designed to sniff out the closest molecules of H_2O within their sensory reach?

It is likely that the mesquite root tip's capacity to form the Deep-State by identifying wet spots in a desert soil is a kind of earnest discernment or sensory intelligence that other trees share as well. It seems that as soon as they discern that a drought is profoundly shaping the desert soils around them, their taproots sense that they should go deeper, quickly growing toward places where caches of residual moisture are more likely to be encountered.

Let's look at it this way: Who wouldn't expect that mesquites, after 25 to 36 million years of living in the deserts and dry subtropics, would have developed the sense to discern where water might be found underground? Being a water witcher or dowser is a rather important skill to have under your belt if lack of moisture is among the most pressing of all the limiting factors that may be shaping your life.

The other talent that mesquite roots have is that of welcoming lots of allies, including arbuscular mycorrhizal fungi and nitrogen-fixing bacteria for starters. As many as thirty-six kinds of arbuscular mycorrhizae have been found in the mycelial networks attached to mesquite roots at just one site.

Over time, their presence helps compensate for the initially low soil fertility found at many of the desert sites that mesquite seedlings colonize. They protect desert soils from erosion, while increasing soil fertility and moisture-holding capacity by shedding off *glomalin,* a glycoprotein that helps bind mineral particles together in fertile soils.

But mycorrhizae do not merely help build the structure or "tilth" in desert substrates; they also help build the very structure of desert plant communities. Most plants in the ancient desert forests occur together in "resource islands," patches of fertility and buffered microclimates that have been bioengineered by the symbiotic relations among mesquite roots and their mycorrhizal allies.

Ecologist Arcadio Monroy Ata and his colleagues have studied these "resource islands" in depth in the dry scrublands dominated by mesquite in central Mexico. Monroy had noticed that mesquites seem to function as a keystone species by building resource-rich mounds in the desert where other species aggregate, just as alligators build nest mounds in the Everglades and bison build buffalo wallows that other species utilize as well. But how do they construct these "resource islands," which often have ten times more nitrogen and other nutrients than can be found in the barren "sea" of sand or silt surrounding them?

What Monroy's team found is that pioneering mesquites often colonize a windswept landscape and begin to lay down roots that break the wind, roots that are soon naturally inoculated with one kind of mycorrhizae and nitrogen-fixing bacteria after another. These multistemmed mesquites then foster the deposition of a mound of fine, windblown soil around their root base, which becomes stabilized by the anchoring root mass and its mycorrhizal hyphae.

As leaf litter and other debris begins to build up the organic matter in the mound, additional kinds of mycorrhizae and their "helper bacteria" find favorable conditions in the root zone. They add many more nutrients and retain much more moisture in these mounds than in the barren interspaces between the mesquite trees. Soon, they have established islands of fertility, moisture, and buffered microclimates ideal for the trapping and germination of windblown seeds of other plant species.

The mesquites, in essence, are practicing *autopoiesis,* a process through which a life form is coupled to a particular physical environment that was once dominated by disturbance. The mesquites and their mycorrhizae then make their "resource island" much more habitable through fostering a chain of ecological interactions that reengineer the physical environment itself.

Curiously, the shared intelligence of the mesquite and the microorganisms attached to its roots "discern" which disturbances to quell and which to enhance in order to create a novel microhabitat—such as the closed-canopy mesquite bosque.

They are doing exactly what Francisco Varela and Humberto Maturana poetically envisioned: The mesquite-mycorrhizae symbiosis "brings forth a world"—its own Deep-State, hidden from our eyes, which then emerges and creates another distinctive microhabitat poised aboveground, in plain sight of all of us.

But what often escapes the eye is that the first "mother" mesquite shares her mycorrhizae with other plant species that live beneath the shelter of her skirts *and also with additional mesquites* that begin to take root in the shelter of the elder mesquite. In this manner, Arcadio Monroy Ata explains, the symbiosis of the elderly mother mesquite and the mycorrhizal fungi on her roots literally *organizes* the structure of the desert vegetation surrounding her first resource island, generating others.

The closer other mesquite trees are to the elder mother, the more mycorrhizal fungi they share and the more habitable their islands become. The outlier mesquites that try to survive on the margins share fewer mycorrhizal species with the trees nearer to the center, but all of their fungal symbionts are probably disseminated by spores or hyphal fragments from the elderly mother as well. Together this spiraling out of trees held in place by mycorrhizae donated by the mother begin to form fractals and crescent-shaped dune fields stabilized in place by the growing mass of taproots, rootlets, and hyphae in the "lower story" or "underworld" of the desert.

Of course, a stabilized mesquite bosque gradually accumulates a guild of shrubs, diverse cacti, and vines in its understory. They, in turn, attract invertebrates, birds, reptiles, mammals, and on occasion amphibians to the nurse plant guild.

All of these interactions could once be seen at the Great Mesquite Forest, a habitat that once covered more than 7 square miles along the Santa Cruz River south of Tucson near Mission San Xavier. As my teachers and mentors Roy Johnson and Ray Turner recently recalled,

The unparalleled avian habitat of the forest was so impressive that descriptions by ornithologists waxed superlative: The exceptional numbers of species [85 kinds of birds, 73 of them nesting], avian densities, number of nests, and the size of trees inspired descriptors using magical or even spiritual terms.

Tens of kinds of hawks and falcons, in addition to caracaras, nine kinds of kingbirds, phoebes, and flycatchers, five owls, four wrens, four doves, three herons, and over a dozen tropical species rarely found in the United States today found ample habitat in the Great Mesquite Forest. But this landscape bioengineered by mesquites and mycorrhizae also harbored at least thirty-nine kinds of mammals, from gray wolves and peccaries to seven bat species and the rare Merriam's mesquite mouse. The Great Mesquite Forest also sheltered thirty-two species of reptiles and amphibians, from lowland leopard frogs and desert tortoises to regal ring-necked snakes and Mexican garter snakes, all rare north of the border today.

In 1994, when I finally took the opportunity to walk all the way through the remnants of the Great Mesquite Forest, it was sadly in tatters. Tragically, groundwater pumping and arroyo cutting had dropped the aquifer there below the root zone of nearly all the mesquites and their remnant mycorrhizae. The Deep-State withered, and then most everyone living aboveground dispersed or died on site.

In essence, one of the most monumental examples of what a diverse mesquite forest has ever been *had died of thirst*. It had become a forest of stumps. Thousands of cars now speed past it on their way from Tucson to the Mexican border each day, without ever realizing the former abundance—the haven for wildlife—that it once nurtured.

But as I zigzagged through the fallen trunks and stumps of its desiccated trees, I could hear something that sounded like the songs of the Ghost Dance rising, echoing off the volcanic mountains in the Tohono O'odham Indian Reservation. Maybe the singing came from a few of the surviving mesquites, their roots vibrating, searching for moisture. Maybe it was from the hoots and hollers of the mycorrhizae beneath my feet, never dead and gone, simply hibernating, patiently waiting.

We will return to our native lands,
We will multiply and flourish once more,
We will emerge from the world below
And arise to grow, flower, and fruit again,
When you least expect us to emerge again.

I suddenly realized that when you fall in love with mesquites, you become wedded to both the living and the doomed, from the smallest flower bud to the largest trunk still barely standing in a bygone forest. They are all yours to love and cherish, dead or alive.

CHAPTER SEVEN

Ghosts

All right, I must concede that perhaps all ghosts don't make good lovers, but it still could be that Ghostly Mesquite Trees do. I mean, it's not like I am shopping for partners per se, but it still might be worth my while to understand how mesquites have fared in their partnerships with others over the years. They remind me of those deliciously sensuous islands of paradise that once existed here in the Snorin' Desert. I recall that an O'odham Indian elder named George Webb once put it this way:

> We never called this place a desert, as if it was impoverished.
> We regarded it as paradise. Paradise.

No doubt George the Elder could see, smell, and taste the many lives that have clustered around mesquite trees in the bosque, where the feasting and frolicking of many creatures, many lovers, had gone on for centuries. But another desert elder I knew once reminded me that mesquites go in and out of relationships, just as humans do. That gave me pause.

When I now look out across a torn and tattered landscape dominated by squat and spindly mesquites—one where giants once grew—I sometimes catch a glimpse of ghosts from that paradise that was sheltered by mesquites. Their love songs still carry in the dry, clear desert air, but so do echoes of their past mournings.

I am speaking of the ghosts of lost loves—the ghosts of evolution —as well as the ghosts of former mentors who guided me into the practice of desert natural history and in the puzzles of evolution.

One moment, I see that life inside the bosque habitat called *mesquital* is still and silent. A moment later, a dust devil has risen up from some disturbance on the desert floor and is raising holy hell, roaring like a banshee and covering everything in its wake with a fine layer of dry talcum powder.

Ghosts take various shapes. Ghosts are chimerical, and for that reason alone, magical. And while not all ghosts are particularly scary, most challenge our ordinary perceptions of how the world works. Or doesn't.

These are the ghosts whom I wish to address.

For the last few days, I have frequently been confronted by the ghost of my old teacher Paul Martin. Paul was a polio victim, a paleoecologist, a palynologist, a prober of pack rat and sloth dung, a passionate proponent of Pleistocene extinctions occurring at the hand of man, and a prolific writer right up until the time of his death.

He was also a man who treated plants as beings of great sensibility. As a man who had difficulty moving at times, he always seemed intrigued by the dynamism, mobility, and sensitivity of plants.

Paul himself was much like a tree, a tall and lanky figure with wild limbs, standing 6 feet 4 inches despite his crippled left leg. It always seemed as if his vision rose up through any canopy, through any ceiling, up, up, and away, out and off to the side.

In other words, Paul was half planted as a heretic and half as a visionary, a hybrid that didn't always sit well with his colleagues. Like an ancient tree, Paul typically took an extremely long view of things, but he did it in a manner that made the *neurotypical* (read *conventional*) colleagues in his forestlike crew think that he was leaning a bit off-center.

I'm sure that many of our neighbors and colleagues dismissed Paul as some kind of crackpot, but I both loved and respected his vision of the deep history of the Snorin' Desert. He was the first scientist I knew who not only studied mesquite, but also tapped into the deeper roots and sensibilities of this desert tree.

By deeper roots, I mean that Paul sought to understand the evolutionary forces that shaped mesquite in its partnerships with others in the landscapes it has coinhabited. Paul and his students were the first to figure that mesquite's distribution range and densities ebbed and flowed with the movements of climate, fire, and the large mammal populations that once roamed this continent.

In doing so, they discerned that mesquites were hardly present anywhere north of the present-day US–Mexico border before the end of the Late Pleistocene "Ice Age" around 12,500 years ago. Our mesquite species now in the lands of the United States were likely "born" (as species) in Mexico. They are "border crossers," we might say, in that they have been firmly settled (and at times unsettled) in both the southwestern United States, and in Mexico.

Of course, that border didn't even exist back then, but I don't think many borders ever existed for Paul Martin anywhere, at any time.

Judging from early pollen depositions and later plant parts found in pack rat dung from Maravillas Canyon Cave in the Big Bend of Texas, Paul reckoned that honey mesquite may have arrived north of the Rio Grande at least thirteen thousand years ago, when now extinct megafauna still roamed the West. It appears that velvet mesquite first appeared in the Waterman Mountains of Arizona a thousand years or so later, spreading up the Gulf of California coast or the many north-south flowing rivers.

Who or what brought them north? Mammoths, mastodons, giant camels, and ground sloths may have had a hand, foot, trunk, or gut in fostering these dispersals, since they were among the potential consumers and defecators of mesquite pods filled with viable seeds ready for germination. They were among mesquite's first vertebrate partners.

Curiously, once these supersize creatures went extinct on the North American continent, the northward dispersal of mesquite into the deserts and semiarid plains from the subtropics seems to have slowed. Paul surmised that it must have taken another five thousand years for sizable velvet mesquite trees to spread through-out the Sonoran Desert and for another form of honey mesquite to form hummocks on the sand dunes near the delta.

Now, while I can hardly remember anything that happened on my first three or four high school dates some fifty years ago (perhaps because nothing did happen), Paul seemed to remember what had happened when mesquite and mammals had their first "dates" ten thousand years ago.

That's about when he found that honey mesquite pods had become relatively common in pack rat nests found in rock shelters at Hueco Tanks, a place that is now a Texas state park east of El Paso. By nine thousand years ago, honey mesquite had been further disseminated up the Rio Grande past the present location of Las Cruces and then north, toward Albuquerque. He once recalled to me that it had more or less spread across the entire Chihuahuan Desert by around eight thousand years ago.

About the time Paul and his collaborators were engaged in this biogeographic detective work, I met him on one of his many trips down to the Research Ranch in Elgin, Arizona.

That's where I had been trying to study the effects of browsing animals on the giant soap tree yuccas of the Sonoita Plain. It must have been around 1975, at a time in my life when I was lonely, bored, and thirsty for some inspiration and intellectual stimulation.

At that moment, I was both at the onset of my wayward career path and on a social trajectory toward oblivion, given that it seemed like there were only two unmarried women in our entire county, with one of them "already engaged" and the other being the sheriff's daughter. I had been living alone for some time, making a meager living raking up tumbleweeds from corrals, painting ranch houses during windstorms, grading roads across boulder fields, and fixing fences regularly cut by heavily armed deer hunters.

For such highly technical work, I was being paid $175 a month, given free board and access to all the yucca flowers and mesquite pods I could eat. But the fringe benefit of this job contract was that I would be granted the chance to meet some of the country's best grassland ecologists, like Paul Martin and his friends Ron Pulliam,

Jane Bock, and Ray Turner. When someone invited me to a small dinner party where this world-famous paleoecologist would be—along with a table full of wines and foods that were well beyond my means—I jumped at the chance to go and meet this Martin guy in the flesh.

I spotted him as soon as I came through the door, a kind of sequoia or redwood, camel or giraffe, who stood above the fray (and the hors d'oeuvres). Not wanting to embarrass myself by making small talk, I went up to Paul and blurted out the most pompous and presumptuous question I could possibly think of.

I asked Paul if he happened to know anything about the evolutionary history of the towering arborescent yuccas and their various and sundry interactions with wildlife past, present, and future . . . in this desert region . . . and in others . . . wherever they occurred on this continent . . . from time immemorial, etc., etc.

Paul looked down at me from his height of 2 meters and forty years of fieldwork, and was silent for a moment . . . well, maybe more than a moment, maybe a minute or two. When he finally spoke, he simply said:

"Well, it's probably not just the contemporary fauna that shaped their stature. I'd bet that when they were emerging from the denser canopies of the subtropics, they were selected for such heights and for the elevated presentation of their fruit by a number of the species in the Pleistocene megafauna."

He took a sip of mescal, then continued:

"Unfortunately, those creatures are no longer physically present to allow us to observe their foraging strategies. Think about it: There are several species of yucca here that display their fruits at heights well out of reach of nearly all living creatures that reach up to eat fruits while keeping all four of their feet firmly planted on the earth . . ."

Then, above the din of all the party talk in the room, he raised his glass, cleared his throat, and shouted out, toasting me:

"Young man, I believe you have your work cut out for you. I suggest that you go and spend the next decade studying all the arborescent *Yucca* species of the subtropics of the Americas if you want to figure out why they are so tall here in the grasslands, and then go to Africa, where a megafauna including giraffes is still intact, and study there. Good luck, my friend."

Everyone in the room was suddenly looking over in our direction, at me, *the little pipsqueak next to Paul.* He might as well have been Paul Bunyan. They all cheered, as if Paul had either just enlisted me as a prospective grad student or banished me to the far reaches of the world for the next twenty years.

I was speechless. I had not yet entertained that possibility as a means to explain what I had been observing in yucca patches, although I had been reading Paul's essays in *Natural History* magazine. One of his widely celebrated articles was about the role he believed humans had played in driving the "charismatic megafauna" of the Ice Age to extinction. I believe the piece later made it into the all-time "best-of" anthology from *Natural History*. It was so audacious, outrageous, and beautifully written that I can still see its pages in my mind's eye ...

The term *megafauna*, of course, simply refers to the "big dogs" on the block, the most charismatic critters to have strutted down the continent since the dinosaurs had checked out, whether they were herbivores, frugivores, carnivores, coprivores, or omnivores. But Paul had a particular interest in the herbivores, frugivores, and coprivores—the grazers, browsers, fruit eaters, and shit eaters—as well as their interactions with *megafloral plants*, like mesquites and yuccas.

"Let others speculate all they want about saber-toothed tigers," he once told me, the single set of species that many paleozoologists were devoted to. "I have enough of a bestiary to deal with for several more lifetimes."

Paul had surmised that before the end of the Ice Age, mesquite pods were massively consumed by giant camelids, hippopotamus- or rhinoceros-size notoungulates, and elephantlike stego-mastodons as they ranged northward out of the subtropical thornscrub. Moreover, Paul hypothesized that these browsers shaped the evolutionary history of mesquites and acacias, along with dozens of other thorny trees with enormous pods or fleshy fruits.

Then, beginning around 11,500 years ago, these mammoth-size creatures began to disappear from the Americas.

By ten thousand years ago, virtually all of those supersize animals had disappeared from North America. As far back as 1780, when Thomas Jefferson described the fossilized bones of a mammoth "six times the size of an elephant" found in Virginia, American naturalists had been debating the causes of the extinction of such mammals.

Paul and his closest colleagues had helped to locate sites where there was detailed evidence of intentional killing of such animals by Paleolithic hunter-gatherers. They mapped the distributions of these killing and processing sites of the megafauna, radiocarbon-dated their bones when they revealed evidence of projectile points or butchering marks, and rescued their enormous turds from dry caves.

––––––––––

Three years later, on the very first day that I had the good fortune of taking a class from Paul, he led us into a lab where we could scratch and sniff at fossilized feces, or *coprolites*, of giant sloths, camels, and bison, ones larger than any of their kin leave on the planet today. He had recently been working on the first-ever paper published in *Science* on what he called *molecular coproscopy*, the inner world of dung.

I had to pinch myself twice before the lab formally began. I had assumed that graduate school could occasionally get interesting, but I had no idea that on my first day in Paul's class, he'd expose me to some "pretty good shit," with twigs and stems as mind-blowing as this stuff.

These "supersize" turds were some of the most prized collections that Paul kept in his paleoecology lab. They were the Who's Who of Scatology. Paul had dissolved many such coprolites in flotation vats full of special chemical solutions, which allowed him to sort the seeds from the chaff the animals had consumed. This not only allowed him to reconstruct their diets but it also offered clues to their past relationships with plants as browsers or grazers.

I was not yet sure I wanted to become a "scat singer" for *my* supper, but then again I was intrigued. Studying past partnerships between plants and mammals by studying dung...hmm... this was the kind of profound psychoanalysis that Sigmund Freud would have swooned over!

Among the many clues that these feces offered up were the pods or seeds of several species of mesquite and catclaw acacia, proof that the plants had once been directly consumed by the megafauna.

Curiously, most seeds in mesquite pods that pass through the gut of a large mammal more or less intact are prone to germinate in the dung the animal leaves behind. But if the pods fall from the tree canopy to the ground or are merely nibbled on by small mammals, they seldom germinate. It took some sleuthing by one of Paul's collaborators, ento-mologist Dan Janzen, to figure out why. Dan was such a probing insect ecologist that it did not take him very long "to meet the beetles."

The pods of mesquite, acacias, and other legumes are typically attacked by bruchid beetles and other seed predators as they begin to ripen on the tree. Most pods that drop to the ground become pockmarked—literally littered—with holes of beetles as they drill and deposit eggs onto the pod or the seeds inside them. Their larvae usually devour enough of the seeds to keep them from ever germinating.

Almost all of the pods that have passed intact through the guts of large mammals have been freed of their seed predators and para-sites. Dan Janzen himself discovered this delicious fact: The beetle larvae are killed by the gastric brew of enzymes and microbiota found in the digestive tracts of many supersize land mammals, but equids especially. And the mesquite seeds that pass through horses and camels seem easier to germinate when their "road apples" are plopped down along a desert trail.

Connie Barlow, a field biologist and science writer from New Mexico, once told me about receiving a "suspicious package" in the mail from Paul. To her relief, it did not smell like woolly mammoth dung. It contained dozens of pods that had fallen from a tree in Tucson where no large herbivores had a chance to devour them. As Connie reported in her fine book, *The Ghosts of Evolution*:

All the pods I received in February were marred by at least one little hole, chewed away by an adult bruchid beetle exiting the pod. Some specimens had a hole over every seed. . . . [In contrast, before they were extirpated], megafauna prevented seed predators and parasites from devastating the crop. . . . By scattering dung over a wide area, fruit-eating mammals help seeds elude seed predators and parasites. Spread out, and sometimes buried deep within dung, the seeds are more difficult to find. In addition, some predators and parasites are deterred by the dung itself. . . . They cannot oviposit on seeds deeply embedded in the dung. . . .

With proof in hand that implied mesquite pods had co-evolved with the gigantic vegetarians of the late Pleistocene, Paul began to hypothesize about the role these animals played in mesquite evolution. He proposed that the thorns on these trees had responded and adapted to these massive foraging machines. They did so in ways that reduced the severity of trampling and branch breakage by the gigantic quadripeds that no doubt relished the pods of mesquite. Alas, many of their branches did get ripped to shreds by these browsing behemoths, so mesquite evolved a tenacious capacity to resprout from the base of its branches and trunks.

Now, this all implies a certain sensitivity of trees like mesquites and acacias to the big hoods in the woods, for the co-evolution of partners is a sensuous dance. Over the years, Paul Martin and his friend Dan Janzen were slowly developing a vocabulary for this reciprocal sensitivity, one that other scientists now embellish and use without much reticence. I can imagine that Paul would be entirely comfortable with the findings of neurobiologists Stefano Mancuso and Alessandra Viola, which appeared in print just a few years after Paul's death in 2010. In *Brilliant Green*, they write that:

Plants have all five senses that humans do: sight, hearing, touch, taste, and smell; each developed in a "plant" way, of course, but no less real. So from this point of view, could we say that they resemble us? Not at all, they're much more sensitive, and besides our five senses, they have at least fifteen others. They sense and calculate gravity, electromagnetic fields, and humidity. And they can analyze numerous chemical gradients.

Paul had surmised that, before their extinction, the coevolutionary dance of mixed herds of megafauna with mesquites dramatically increased the stem density of mesquite near waterholes. At the same time, it is possible that their browsing and trampling—among other factors—kept in check the expansion of mesquite into surrounding habitats. Of course, some viable seeds would be dispersed in their feces as they traveled to the edges of other springs, seeps, or lakes, but cooler winters during that era may have also prevented the ubiquity of mesquite during the Late Pleistocene.

By Paul's way of thinking, the megafauna had coevolved with mesquite in numerous ways. *In fact, they had helped bring mesquite to its senses!*

Prior to their extinction, these browsers' affinity for legumes had profoundly influenced the very shapes and sensitivities of mesquite trees, the size and sweetness of their pods, their capacity to resprout or to survive germination in dung, and their geographic distribution. Mammoths and sloths are gone from our midst, but their influence on mesquite and acacias lingers on, especially at the desert's edge.

Connie Barlow aptly calls these ecological anachronisms "the ghosts of evolution," for their features seem nonsensical if we try to explain them by looking only at their interactions with the present wildlife of desert regions. Instead we must look into the deep history of their relationships, especially their past partnerships with bygone megafauna.

If you were not at all aware of their missing partners, the mesquite pods, yucca fruits, Osage oranges, pawpaws, giant prickly pears, and calabash trees would seem more like monstrosities that a pot-smoking Dr. Seuss had invented for an islandlike world of his own, rather than species marvelously fitted to the arid subtropical expanses of the Americas.

Soon after my first dinner and then first class with Paul, my favorite Lebanese-American aunt called me long distance, something she had never done before. She told me that she had "airmailed" me some recent newspaper clippings from the *National Enquirer*, the place all my relatives turned to in order to catch up on the latest scientific discoveries and debates.

She had sent me all the articles she could find about a "nutty professor" named Dr. Martin as a way to warn me away from such weirdos. The newspaper articles implied that Paul was a mad scientist because he asked the federal government to spend millions putting out a fire in Rampart Cave, down in the Grand Canyon. The fire was consuming the dung balls of the extinct Shasta giant ground sloth that Paul and his colleague Austin Long had meticulously studied.

When the fire was discovered, Paul had called a press conference. He wanted to alert decision makers of the scientific value of those smoldering deposits of Shasta sloth dung with mesquite seeds embedded in them. He referred to the dung in the cave as "priceless ecological archives" equivalent in value to all the books in the Library of Congress, including the Bible.

Apparently, my auntie was not amused. A few days after the clippings arrived in the mail, my aunt made another of her rare long-distance calls to me from her home in Indiana.

"Did you read those stories I sent about that madman running loose on your campus, honey?" my Aunt Rose said.

"What madman? Oh, Paul? Well, he actually can't run very easily, given the condition of his leg," I answered.

"So you actually know this nutty professor who is wasting all our taxpayers' money studying prehistoric BS?"

"Well, it's not really BS, auntie. Some of it is MS, for mammoth shit, some of it is SS, for sloth shit. Or SGSS, really, since it is Shasta ground sloth shit. It's like aged wine; it just keeps getting more valuable as time goes on."

She cackled.

When I told her that I was indeed studying with Paul, there was a long silence. Then a kind of disgusted moan flowed out of my phone receiver.

"Don't you know how hard your parents worked to give you a good education? And you're going to waste it all to study with someone who is trying to save old dinosaur poop from burning up?"

"Well, it's not actually poop from dinosaurs, Auntie," I replied. "It's from Pleistocene megafauna. And don't worry, it doesn't smell much anymore, given that it's been thousands of years since it was dumped in the cave. In fact, coprolites are typically rather hard to the touch, just like any fossil—"

"I just don't care what you call it. It is still *poop*. Keep your hands off of it."

My dearest aunt hung up on me, entirely unimpressed with my sojourn into scatology with Paul as my mentor.

Thankfully, she never brought up all that crap again.

It was not until years after I met him that I realized Paul's gift could not easily be separated from his disability, and that such a statement might be true for me in my quest to become treelike as well. (I bet it's true for most of us, although I have collected so many flaws and dysfunctions that it's hard to gift-wrap them anymore.)

For Paul, the Mexican strain of the polio virus that had severely stricken his left leg earlier in life forced him to look at everything off to the side, a vantage point different from that of other scientists. Metaphorically and figuratively, he towered above his peers like the Banyan tree off-kilter, or the Leaning Tower of Pisa. For me, hanging out with Paul was like spending time with the Abraham Lincoln of field biologists. There was both a brilliance and a certain errant quality to just about everything he said.

Years later, when I shared a day with Paul in Alamos, Sonora, he reminded me why mesquite mattered to him so very much. Our friend Sandy Lanham—a bush pilot of great skill and daring—had taken Paul up in her little plane that morning to survey the cliffs that formed a transition zone between the deserts and the tropics. He was still in awe of what he had seen just after the first dawn light, because it was such rugged country that he would never be able to walk far back into it.

Before he even fully greeted me, he said:

"You know, Gary, I really love this place, this ecological edge. I can finally see how our Sonoran Desert flora emerged right out of the tropical deciduous forests and subtropical thornscrub that runs from here all the way down to Costa Rica in one unbroken chain. And while dozens of acacias dominate the lowlands to the south of here, it is mesquite—not the few acacias that moved northward with them—that dominate the deserts from here on up to the Grand Canyon. The mammoths, mastodons, camels, giant asses, and sloths could have so easily carried them northward, savoring their sweet, fat, juicy pods much more than the dry papery pods of our spindly little acacias."

He continued:

"Perhaps that's why we found so many mesquite seeds in the dung balls of Shasta ground sloths up in the Grand Canyon—they are among the northernmost expression of the fruits the gomphotheres and ground sloths ate all the way down through the subtropics."

Paul gazed up toward the cliffs and crest of the volcanic hills behind me, where the desert and the tropics intersected. I cast my own eyes downward, because I realized he had made me see for the very first time the ghosts that had long haunted him. He noticed I was silent.

At last he spoke up: "Gary, how are you doing? I heard that you've recently gone through a breakup, you know, a separation from your wife."

I was as embarrassed to talk to him about my current dilemma as I was the first time I tried to talk with him at the Research Ranch party twenty years earlier.

"Well, Paul, I guess I felt we just weren't growing in the same direction anymore. I dunno, maybe she felt exhausted or overshadowed by me, like we were competing or something. I never felt that way, but I did get claustrophobic around her family, like there was no place in the room for me . . . "

My mouth got dry, and I stopped talking.

Paul was silent for a while. Then he pointed out into some vegetation and started talking as if he were explaining an ecological field problem.

"Do you see those two trees over there, right at the base of the next ridge over?" Paul asked me. I thought that he was abruptly changing the subject, as if he regretted making any mention of my still-open wound.

"Here, take my field glasses; look at that pair of trees. Now think about them, their history there. They probably germinated about the same time, within a few feet of one another, and grew side by side at the same pace for a good number of years.

"But then, after a point, one is shading out the other for part of the day, and vice versa. They may be competing for nutrients. Or the ants on one are cutting a little branch off the other when it crosses their path . . .

"Is it any wonder that they start growing in different directions, seeking out the sun? But what a wonderful miracle it is that they grew in tandem, peaceably, for so many years.

"Savor that, Gary. Savor the memory of all the years you grew in pace together, side by side."

Paul's digression from talking about vegetation to talking about human relationships at first seemed like a radical detour to me, one that again embarrassed me. I just couldn't respond to it at that time.

As I later thought back on that brief but poignant conversation, I realized that he, like most of the best ecologists I know, had a hard time unhitching one part of the world from another. He metaphorically used the structure of ecological relationships to help him understand human relationships, and vice versa. For Paul, there were few tangents that did not reveal something about the core issues of life. And with his guidance, I learned that there was not much difference between the growth trajectories of me and a tree.

During the last trip I ever took with Paul, he seemed to be having a post-polio syndrome rebound, which made it increasingly difficult for him to walk with just a cane. Soon he would need crutches or a walker, and later, a motorized wheelchair.

But for the moment, Paul was back at one of those fascinating tension zones, called *ecotones*, between the deserts and tropics, this time near Gomez Farias, Tamaulipas, where he had done the field-work for his master's thesis a half century earlier.

"It must feel great to be here again," I said, as we arrived at the edge of a deep gorge. A somewhat deteriorated suspension bridge of rotting wooden slats and two guy wires stood between us and the other side of the gorge. I assumed that we could go no farther. We'd savor the moment of being right smack dab on the Tropic of Cancer.

"What do you mean 'great to be here again'? We're not *here* yet. My thesis sites were on the other side of the gorge. I'd like to go across."

My Mexican friends looked at him like he was crazy, given the condition of the bridge and his own leg. Then they looked at me as if I could, or would, try to stop him. Before any of us could speak, Paul dropped his cane and lumbered out onto the suspension bridge, which was already swaying wildly with his every move. We watched in disbelief as he placed his good leg forward, grasped onto the waist-high cables above the bridge, and swung his other leg sideways to move it forward, rocking the bridge as he went.

It took him five minutes to cross over and another eight to return. His shirt was drenched in sweat and his face was beet red, but Paul was grinning from ear to ear. It was as if he had crossed over some geographic gap like the Bering Land Bridge, just as some of the megafauna had done many thousands of years ago.

"I just had to do that," he said, panting. "I had to know I could still do that."

To still do that—to cross over to a place that not many other people would ever care to know, let alone venture to. That is why Paul Martin is one of the ghosts who will haunt me for the rest of my life. I sit under a mesquite and read a few passages of his last book, *Twilight of the Mammoths: Ice Age Extinctions and the Rewilding of America,* as if it is another rickety suspension bridge he laid out before us, spanning what seems to be an uncrossable chasm between the past and the future.

Paul wanted us all to move into a deeper understanding of and love for ecological history, to reach into a richer way of looking at the world. He wanted that deep history to knock us off balance—to knock our socks off—so that we could imagine a richer, not a more impoverished, future for ourselves and our descendants and all other creatures as well. He was never concerned about how hazardous the journey would be, or how many perils he or you or I might face along the way. He just knew that we had to try to get to the other side.

―――――――――――

And now, I too felt I was headed to the other side. For me, there was still this strong desire not just to study mesquites, but to become one. Or one with it. In some kind of deeper relationship.

CHAPTER EIGHT

Revival

I had not yet gone out in public since I had begun my metamorphosis into mesquite-hood. I feared that the people around me might notice the nodules and hyphae crowding out of my huaraches, and the extra-floral nectaries forming ever so subtly in my armpits. I worried that the skin on my forearms was becoming a bit barklike, and that too many phainopeplas were dropping their sticky seeds onto me.

But when Laurus suggested that we join the largest gathering of mesquite lovers in the Stinkin' Hot Desert, I could not refuse. I needed to be around some folks who adored mesquite trees as much as we did. They might not be able to recognize that I was hell-bent on becoming one with/of the mesquites, but they surely shared with me the feeling that mesquites were the objects of our affection. And, on the chance that I could not fully be transformed into a tree, at least I could dwell among other treehuggers who would not be put off at all by my obsession with this woody legume.

And so I consented, but I decided to wear an extra-large cowboy hat to conceal the phainopepla nest materials in my hair and socks under my huaraches to contain my ever-more-tangled root hairs, hyphae, and nodules.

But as soon as we arrived at the Mesquite Festival in Tucson, I breathed a sigh of relief, for it was clear that I would be among kindred sprouts:

MESQUITE

"It's time to get a legume up on life, Mesquiteers!" I heard the master of ceremonies bark out.

Today Laurus and I are delighted that we have joined a motley crew of some three thousand Mesquiteers gathering together for one of Tucson's most favorite autumn orgies (of vegetal sorts). No, they are not having tailgate parties just before a football game nor are they trick-or-treating for UNICEF. Oddly, they have not congregated to celebrate a holiday nor to lament a holocaust. The celebrity figure for their festival is neither saint nor sinner, but a sinewy senior floral member of their own community.

Today, mesquite is at center stage. (*Take a bough!*) The masses have gathered today to pledge arboreal allegiance; to celebrate the miracles associated with that nearly saintlike nitrogen fixer, that luscious legume, that frisky phreatophyte. They wish to redeem the status of this wild and woody perennial. We are attending Tucson's annual Mesquite Festival, so that we might better learn how to attend to this tree.

It is mid-November, and yet it is still warm and sunny in the Dunbar/Spring barrio just a mile from the heart of historic Tucson. Residents of the sprawling desert city still call it the Old Pueblo. It holds archaeological evidence of more than four thousand years of continuous farming and foraging in its midst. That is one of several distinctions that has recently earned Tucson a United Nations designation as the first UNESCO City of Food Cultures in the United States.

Mesquite trees might want to stand and wave to their admirers for the role they played in Tucson receiving that honor. They have been the most important of all wild food plants ever foraged from the Snorin' Desert in and around the Tucson Basin. Over the decades, centuries, and millennia, they consistently provided more calories to the indigenous inhabitants of the Tucson Basin than corn had ever offered to humans in such a desert clime.

But most of the contemporary residents of Tucson have forgotten that, as if they were suffering from an epidemic of GA—Gastronomic Alzheimer's—that had made them lose interest in most every food put on their plate before the inventions of Hapless Meals and Microshocked Pizzas. As my friend Tim Weed puts it, most Arizonans "don't even peel *nopal* [cactus pads] no more."

Of course, for every current, there is a countercurrent. You might say that Laurus and I had finally bonded with our very own Mesquite Splinter Group. Those of us who decided to come together at the Mesquite Festival might well have been the largest gathering of *Prosopis* promoters in the history of humankind. You might say that we have come out of our closets to attend the annual meeting of the Sacred Order of Unconditional Lovers of Mesquite Trees.

We suddenly realized that we were not alone. *We were in a forest of friends.*

Of course, much of the time, the mesquite still goes unnoticed and unloved as it goes about its duties of serving our community. Its humility is such that it seldom even claims to be a tree, for it is just as happy being called a shrub, a bush, a switch, a simple member of the *monte* or desert scrublands that carpet much of this Land of Little Rain.

Regardless of its often diminutive stature, mesquite looms larger in the hearts, minds, and bellies of us border anarchists. For the last decade, it has been annually honored here at this community festival, which persuasively reminds local residents of mesquite's many values and uses, as well as recounting the many former abuses it has suffered.

The Tenth Anniversary Mesquite Festival was destined to become one of the best and largest ever hosted by the Desert Harvesters, a group that might be likened in their fervor to the Harry Potter tribe or to Deadheads. Other than being certifiably loco for legumes, they are an impassioned and intelligent collective of wild food foragers who live primarily in the Snorin' Desert. They include individuals who have spent years championing the renewed use of a variety of wild native foods that grow side by side with mesquite trees or beneath the same canopy cover: cholla cactus buds, *quelite* greens, and *bellota* acorns.

The Desert Harvesters assert that these are the foods that we will survive upon after the Aquifer-Depleting Apocalypse. They can be produced on only six drops of rain and the single flashflood or snowstorm that the desert annually provides. For this reason, mesquite is their manna.

Many of our fellow Desert Harvesters proudly accept the moniker of "*wild* foragers" in reference to themselves, and not just in reference to the native plants they put on their tables. Believe me, this crew is a resourceful bunch. They've figured out how to take dust baths and use waterless toilets. These guys know how to throw great pool parties without even needing to get wet. Some of them even attend the all-night orgies of lickable toads that unexpectedly appear when a whopper summer thunderstorm makes the streams flow for the first time in a gazillion years.

This year, Laurus and I are present at the festival not merely as gawkers and consumers. We are posing as migrant workers promoting the fire-roasted mesquite flour produced by our dear friends in the Seri Indian community 400 miles south of Tucson. But we are also taking the helm of the Taco Diplomacy Food Wagon, a mobile art and education exhibit made of mesquite planks created by the talent in the Sabores sin Fronteras Foodways Alliance. Our motto: Walk the Taco. Two-Step Your Way Right across the Line. (With hands across the border, a taco is in order!)

And yet, if you observed our body language, you might notice that Laurus and I appear as though we are stunned, if not shell-shocked, by finding so many kindred spirits in one place. And we are enormously grateful and surprised by the many ingenious ways our community has been embracing mesquite and its myriad products.

These treehuggers really know how to squeeze a tree for all it's worth.

When I first moved to Tucson more than thirty-five years ago, a festival like this to celebrate mesquite would have gone over like the proverbial fava bean in church. In the old days—*aquel tiempo*—it was more likely for my neighborhood to host a boat race in a dry wash, like the one we called the Little Rillito River Regatta. Or we'd gather publically only for the annual cholla cactus joint toss, where we'd pass around a few cactus joints for good measure as well. Simply put, in those days, mesquites got no respect from either the rural or the urban sectors of borderlands society. At best, they were considered firewood.

Nothing like having your entire image and societal value based on being dead: dead wood.

Back then, mesquite trees were blatantly abused. I could feel their pain, but hardly knew what to do. There were hardly any plants rights activists back then.

I can still remember how they were disparaged and vilified.

I recall that a rancher from Northwest Texas, W. T. Waggoner, once indicted mesquite trees with this curse: "It's the devil with roots, it scabs my cows, spooks my horses, and gives little shade."

Ah, yes, it was as if a mesquite was Lucifer made manifest in the Legume Family. The Devil in the Woodpile, as an old song goes.

I am suddenly reminded of mesquite's days of suffering low esteem by an elderly woman who has come up to our Taco Diplomacy Food Wagon to check it out. She is in festive regalia, with faintly bluish hair and Western-style cowgirl attire. I am perched there in the wagon, hawking 1-pound bags of sweet flour ground from the sun-dried pods of honey mesquite. The wagon itself is made of thick planks cut from velvet mesquite trunks salvaged from trees in a desert area bulldozed for highway widening just north of Tucson.

I watch as the elderly lady touches the richly colored boards, lightly sweeping her thin, bony fingers around the swirls of a blonde knot in the midst of dark red and brown rings revealed by cutting the tree trunk into boards. She picks up a bag of mesquite pod flour.

She slowly reads on the label that its pods were harvested by Seri Indian hunter-gatherers who live half a day's drive south into Mexico.

She sets the bag back down on the counter and pauses thoughtfully.

She then tips the brim of her straw cowgirl hat up so that I can see her pale blue eyes peeking out from wrinkled, suntanned cheeks. They are laughing, dancing eyes. This elder is clearly bemused.

"Well, I'll *be*. I'll be damned. I'll be *damaged*. *Eating* mesquite. Imagine *that*. I can tell you one thing for sure. When I was growin' up, they didn't pick nor eat the beans off any mesquite tree. They *poisoned* them trees. They dragged them down with chains running between two bulldozers, driving in tandem across the range. They grubbed those suckers out of the ground until their roots was upright, danglin' in the dry air.

"Where I grew up near Big Springs, Texas, no one could even imagine a bunch of people fawnin' over a mesquite tree, let alone eatin' its beans. If anything, them was for hungry heifers and their dogies during those drought years, that's about all they was considered good for. *My, how times change.*"

They do, indeed, change. Sometimes, for the good.

My CowHippy compadre—Southern Arizona rancher Dennis Moroney—agrees with us that the views of mesquite in the stockmen's community have indeed shifted:

> There used to be only one question about mesquite being asked in the West: What means should we use to destroy this plant? Fire? Mechanical control? Chemical control? But today there is really no reason to ignore the many benefits of mesquite any longer. It offers fertility, fuel, and food. Forage, shade, and windbreaks. Flood control and sometimes even flood mitigation. And some of the finest honey, flooring, and furniture in the world. . . .
>
> It seems like it's time we made our peace with mesquite.

It was true enough. Even when I began to apprentice myself to mesquites at the age of twenty-three, I too knew that mesquite was not the blessed sight for most Arizonans that it was for me. And yet I knew a few innovative minds who could already see mesquite in a different light.

Still, I could hardly work up the courage to tell some of my neighbors that I made my (meager) living wandering barefoot across the desert floor at dawn, tallying up the number of ripe mesquite pods per tree. If I had argued with them that the mesquite forests deserved some modicum of protection, they would have hoisted me up in a Hangin' Tree.

In other words, I had good reason to be a *clandestine* bean counter . . . or pod counter, actually. I had not yet come out of the mesquite wood-paneled closet. But I already knew I was going against the grain.

No doubt my neighbors believed that both this tree and I had fallen from grace. They likely feared we had gone over to the Dark Side of the Desert Forest.

Needless to say, even today people are not of one mind about mesquite in the Southwest. We have been historically infected by some sort of leguminous schizophrenia. It's even spread into patches of Mexico and other parts of the world where *Prosopis* grows, from Honolulu to Ouagadougou.

Mesquite has come to divide the treehuggers from the graziers from the hatchet men. But it's not like separating the seed from the chaff, or pitting good against evil in some primordial passion play. Each of these groups has its virtues and its varmints, its assets and its asses.

To some extent, the Mesquite (Culture) Wars have continued unabated unto this very day. To the north of my present home in Patabutta, a few ranchers still wrap them in chains and grub many of the shrubby sort out of the ground, while judiciously leaving a few good-sized trees for shade and browse. I don't mind such practices all that much, as long as the wood goes into fireplaces or furniture, which it does in this case.

But to the west of me some fifty miles, I once walked through a ghostly patch of dead mesquite trunks where the Bureau of Indian Affairs had aerially sprayed the desert vegetation with the same herbicides that had been used to defoliate the jungles of Vietnam. Thank God, most of those herbicide treatments did not work all that well, for the bushes resprouted within a couple years, so most ranchers abandoned that practice. But what, if any, was the impact on the health of the native foragers who gathered firewood and the edible pods of the mesquites sprayed there?

What that elderly cowgirl from the Lone Star State had alluded to was true. She had minced no words. She was absolutely correct in admitting that a War of the Woods has raged like a wildfire from here clear to Car-Nation. Some of the mercenaries in that war have been hell-bent on annihilating mesquite, but they had no better luck than US troops did in North Vietnam or Afghanistan.

I am not disparaging our troops. I'm just conceding that our political readers have misread the landscape and put lives at risk by doing so.

Isolated skirmishes still and will flare up from the Chihuahuan Desert lands of West Texas to the Mohave in Southern California. Mesquite trees have been subjected to chainsaw massacres, bulldozer scrapings, tar-and-featherings, drownings in motor oil, controlled burns, and Agent Orange spraying frenzies on hundreds of thousands of acres, as if they were no more than worthless weeds.

And yet here we are, me and that elderly cowgal from Big Springs, shaking hands and hugging, four decades after the war on mesquite reached its zenith. We both are glad it is behind us. And now we are surrounded by dozens of Mesquiteers of all ages who are poised to purchase oodles of mesquite flour, jelly, and honey.

But so many people from all walks of life at this Mesquite Festival are not present simply to partake in a feeding frenzy. Some of them pray that mesquite's nutrients and chemoprotective substances will keep their diabetes and heart disease at bay. Others consider its timber to be our highest-quality wood for crafting guitars or smoking bison meat for barbecue. Still others hold out the hope that it will become our greatest ally in sequestering carbon to slow the rate of global climate change.

Hope. Mesquite offers us a *politics of hope*. It offers us the opportunity to finally come to peace with the landscapes we have inherited, to live productively with them, rather than constantly trying to give those landscapes a makeover so that they will look and behave like someone else's place. It offers to reconcile us with our rangy neighbors on the range. We are all tilting toward some angle of repose where we can live and let live, if not love the mesquite. It grows up out of the "radical center" of the West, a place where ranchers and environmentalists are joining hands to define a more peaceable future. But make no mistake about it: This tree does not grow in an economic or social vacuum, as my mesquite pod–casting wife often reminds me. One man's fish is another man's "poisson."

Nor is the Desert Harvesters' Mesquite Festival solely about the economic value of this xerophytic shrub. I would assert that it is an indicator of the early onset of *xerophilia*—the contagion of love for, of, and in the desert.

In fact, the festival foments a broader expression of xerophilia, an unconditional love that embraces all that punctures, pricks, sticks, and stings. From the window of the Taco Diplomacy Food Wagon, I see vendors selling syrups, soaps, jams, fruit leathers, and barbecue sauces made from the fruits of the giant saguaro cactus and the lowly prickly pear. Others are offering the desert's most potent healing herbs such as creosote, range ratany, limber bush, and yerba mansa in potions, plasters, tinctures, teas, and salves. Still others market raw foodstuffs or dried spices gathered from the desert floor—from Sonoran oregano to chia seeds—for all these plants grow amidst the mesquite-studded hillsides and floodplains of the desert borderlands.

We have come to learn that over the centuries, our predecessors and ancestors found ways to gather these healing herbs into medicine bundles, cabinets, pantries, and larders where mesquite gums and saps, meals and seeds, had also been cached.

In short, this love fest for mesquite is both a Woodstock and a Feedstock for the Snorin' Desert as a whole. As I pause and listen, I hear O'odham Indian fiddle music in the air, drowning out the drone and thump and putter of hammer mills as they pulverize mesquite pods into the finest of flours. A half dozen more millers have shown up with their machinery to grind the pods that participants have harvested over the previous months gratis. And because of all the roasting and milling being done on the spot, the barrio air is sweet and smoky.

———————

This particular Sunday morning, I found solace in the fact that a few thousand mesquite lovers have come out of their closets to the Dunbar/Spring Community Garden on the edge of Barrio Anita to redeem the reputation and the dignity of their Sweet Heartwood-of-a-Tree. I am but one of many who has come out of my reluctance to fully and publicly embrace mesquites as partners in this arboreal journey across the desert. We are coming out of the closet—legume-kind and humankind together—out into the bril-liant burning sunshine of our desert home.

It is a fitting moment for us to remember that before mesquite's fall from grace a half century or so ago, this tree had provided more than three hundred generations of desert residents with food, shel-ter, fuel wood, fence posts, furniture, utensils, sealants, charcoal, and topical and internal medicines. It is time for us to recognize that *Prosopis* has provided building materials for prehistoric pit houses, wattle-and-daub sandwich houses, *jacales,* and adobes, as well as for chicken coops, storage sheds, outhouses. mailboxes, trophy homes, and sacred altars.

Perhaps we need this kind of Leguminous Love Fest to remind ourselves how much our region's human history is entwined with the limbs of mesquite trees. In the late 1850s, Lieutenant Edward Beale was the first writer of note to admit his attraction to the mes-quite. At that moment, Beale was leading the ill-fated Camel Corps of the US Army as it traversed the North American deserts from the coast of the Gulf of Mexico all the way across the Sun Belt to the coast of California. On the way, he fell in love, as I have recently done, with a tree that is a real head turner.

Remarkably, Beale prophesied that making the most of mesquite would become key to the "settling" of the West. While his inten-tions were noble and his hope for a new "mesquite culture" laudable, Beale was a wee bit too far ahead of his time.

At last, mesquite's own redemptive song has clearly begun to be sung. Recently, even the mass media has taken note. Twitters and Fritters, in Mesquite Podcasts and on the Wood-Wide Web, report that mesquite smoke has surpassed hickory smoke (and hashish?) as America's most popular aromatic flavoring in barbe-cue sauces, marinades, potato chips, dips, Cheetos, Fritos, Doritos, and burritos.

The patina of mesquite's wood has become legendary among all manner of furniture shapers, guitar makers, and undertakers. Its pod flour and its tortillas can now be found for the first time ever in communion wafers for the Blessed Sacrament, on the shelves of Whole Foods grocereterias, and in raw foods kiosks of Paleo-Diet

Cave Man cafeterias. And as I write this, it could be that someone is placing it in a space capsule so that it can become the first Legume on the Moon.

But as Laurus and I leave the festival, I mull over the fact that being present there has raised a slew of knotty questions for me: Am I getting into a relationship of unrequited love, or are the feelings reciprocal? Will Prosopis juliflora *be jealous of my unflinching allegiance to* Laurus nobilis, *the human love of my life? And how do I feel about the fact that Mesquite has so many other lovers?*

Given its former affairs with Phainopepla and Mistletoe, will our relationship have any legal standing? If we travel together, will Mesquite be carded at the border, arrested and deported, then forced to stay behind? If we try to flee from our repressive government by air, will mesquite's trunks be searched? Will they fit into the overhead compartments on the plane? Will authorities recognize me as its wood-be lover?

And what will the authorities do with me if I try to metamorphose any further? Will I be barred from using certain outhouses in the Carolinas? Do I still want to be transformed into a tree that is still so disparaged, denigrated, and denuded throughout so much of its range? Does the heartwood of all mesquites have fatal flaws that I cannot yet see?

And other, deeper (or dumber) philosophical questions began to nag at me as well: Does it really matter whether mesquite trees care for me as much as I care for them? Does the history of humankind's relationship with mesquite tell us more about ourselves—who we are and who we have been—than anything about the mesquite tree itself?

To answer these questions, I feel I might need to carefully consider the mental, emotional, spiritual, and nutritional health of others who have fallen in love with mesquite or who have been transformed into one of its kind. The answers might be different from those I might get by interviewing Prosopis *alone.*

CHAPTER NINE

Nourishment

I must confess that my love for and curiosity about mesquite have taken me to places I had never thought to venture before, to speak with others whose lives I might have unnecessarily overlooked. I was beginning to feel that I had become a contortion artist, being twisted up every which way for the love of a tree. Of course, the fun of being in love is seeing where it takes you—to places that you wouldn't otherwise visit . . .

But I was beginning to feel that Laurus nobilis *was not amused by my obsession with mesquite. One day she asked me:*

"Can't you just go out and study some plant that isn't edible for a while? It seems that whenever we sit down together, mesquite is already at the dinner table. I feel like I might be beginning to gain weight from all the mesquite goodies that you and your research team are making, and I'm sure that you are gaining weight eating all those mesquite muffins . . . I think you need to get away from all this for a while . . . go to where there are maple trees or redwoods instead . . ."

I moaned, then tried to stutter out an answer:

"B-but I like hanging out with others who are about my height . . . Maples? Redwoods? . . . They're just way too tall. I don't want to be with tall trees who look down on me all the time . . ."

"Why don't you take a little trip then, away from velvet mesquites, to gain a little perspective. Take a time-out. Why don't you hang out for

a while with some of our friends who are archaeologists, rather than all these chefs and bakers and brewers and distillers . . . ?"

"Well, I do know some archaeologists in Texas that work with the other mesquites . . . and with acacias. Dead ones, mind you. I could go see them . . ."

Laurus nodded with approval, and then added, "But no cheating, do you hear? Leave all your pretty little mesquite muffins in the freezer. Let them chill out, okay?"

"Okeydokey," I replied.

I saddled up my aging Prius named Ol' Paint and headed for the Land of the Honey Mesquite, Prosopis glandulosa, *along the Rio Grande. What I didn't mention to Laurus was that I had another motivating factor in mind for this trip: to understand the different ways that mesquite has been in relationship with humans over time. In essence, I was asking, "Has mesquite ever been married to humans in a manner different than how we normally think about matrimony and domestication?"*

My trip didn't exactly start out with a sharp focus on matrimony . . . instead, it seemed that I was back on the manure trail, or as my Mexican buddies call it, *la ruta de mierda.* I went to Big Bend to refamiliarize myself with the story of mesquite seeds found in fossilized feces along the Rio Grande in Texas. That's what the likes of Vaughn Bryant and E. O. Callen discovered decades ago in human coprolites from South Texas and the adjacent Mexican state of Tamaulipas. They opened our eyes to the antiquity of mesquite in human diets . . . and in human relationships . . . even if we had to close our nostrils to this fact at the very same time.

I had particularly clued in to Vaughn Bryant's work when we spent a week together years ago in an archaeological retreat along the Rio Grande near Lajitas, Texas. Curiously, Bryant's discoveries of the antiquity of honey mesquite in human diets came from the very same stretch of the Rio Grande in which mesquite was first recorded as a staple by the earliest known visitors from the Old World to the deserts of the New World. In all likelihood, the historic campsite that these pilgrims visited in July 1535 is now buried under the waters of the Falcon Reservoir on the lower Rio Grande.

Nevertheless, we are fortunate to have a "glimpse at" what a prehistoric mesquite-grinding party was like, thanks to a testimony offered by the Spanish explorer Alvar Nuñez Cabeza de Vaca. His 1,500-mile journey across the deserts was set down on paper several years after he returned to Mexico City around 1535:

After we parted from those whom we left weeping, we went with the others to their dwellings. And those who were in the dwellings received us very graciously. They brought us their children who put out their hands to offer us flour of *mesquiquez*. This *mesquiquez* is a pod that when it is on the tree is very bitter and is like carob beans [*algarrobas*] and is eaten with earth and with this it is sweet and good to eat.

The way they treat it is like this: They make a pit in the ground to a depth that each one wants, and after they have thrown the pods into this pit, with a wooden mortar as thick as a leg or an arm and half as long as a limb, they mash the pods until they are ground into a very fine flour.

In addition to the particles of soil already in the pit that stick to the ground-up mesquite flour, they toss into the pit additional handfuls of clay when they are ready to grind more pods. After the grinding is done, they throw this mixture into a basket-like container and sprinkle it with water, which initially pools on top of the flour before being absorbed.

At that point, the person who ground the mixture samples its taste and if it seems to him that it is not yet sweet enough, he asks for more clay to mix in. He does this again and again until he is satisfied with its sweetness. He then gathers all the people to seat themselves around the pit, and each one puts their hand into the vessel to scoop out and sort what he can, separating the flour from the seeds and chaff that is thrown on hides placed nearby. The miller than picks up all the partially ground pod fragments, returns them to the vessel, pours water on them, and then squeezes out a sweet juice, tossing the remaining solids on the hides once more. In this manner, they make three or four preparations of food or drink at each grinding. For those who have been invited to the feast, they consider this a very great event, for they come away with their bellies full of all the flour, clay, and water they have consumed.

Guided by some of Bryant's insights, I wish to reveal to you several fascinating clues hidden in this passage.

Clue number one: The addition of fine clay to remove the bitterness or minor toxins from foods was a widespread practice in desert areas and is known by the euphonious name of *geophagy*, literally "earth eating."

Clue number two: The native mesquite miller's use of a wooden mortar—one likely made of dense mesquite wood—was common along a stretch of the middle and lower Rio Grande, where rock types suitable for making grindstones and mortars were unavailable.

Clue number three: The removal of bitterness with clay and further leaching through squeezing the pod fragments in water suggests that the mesquite being consumed was either from a relatively bitter population of honey mesquite or from the less common screwbean mesquite. Similar processing techniques for screwbean mesquite were recorded as being still intact among the Gila River Pima Indians in Arizona around 1900. Indeed, they were widely used by dozens of cultures all across the American Desert for millennia.

My own first taste of a mesquite "pudding" processed in roughly this same manner occurred on Thanksgiving Day among the Gila River Indian Community of Akimel O'odham, or Pima. We were gathered at the Ruth and Joe Giff residence in the Pima rancheria of Komatke, a few miles south of Phoenix, Arizona. We were fancying ourselves as Thanksgiving eaters of what Arizona residents would have eaten before the Pilgrims arrived on the other side of the continent.

And so, it is somewhat odd that some historians attribute the so-called discovery of the value of mesquite by Europeans to Cabeza de Vaca or to Hernando de Alarcón, another explorer of his era. While Cabeza de Vaca recorded eating mesquite in the country now called Texas, it was likely that his sidekick Estevanico el Negro was more engaged in this encounter than Cabeza de Vaca was. Estevanico was the one who likened mesquite to the edible carob pods of his home ground, probably being among the first to use the Arabic name *algarroba* for it.

Estevanico, also known as Mustafa al Zemmouri, was a black African slave from Morocco who had survived a terrible drought in his homeland by foraging for wild foods like carob pods when he was a boy.

Nevertheless, it's a rather silly exercise to decide who from the Old World—Alvar, Hernando, or Estevanico—should be credited with "discovering" mesquite's food value. Given that the indigenous peoples had been eating from this tree of life for upward of six millennia, this is a little like deciding whether to give Peter Piper or Chuck E. Cheese credit for popularizing pizza in America.

To offer the "head" of their crew some credit, Cabeza de Vaca realized that eating mesquite had survival value for both desert hunter-gatherers and subsistence farmers alike. There can be little doubt that he and three other pilgrims—Estevanico, Andrés Dorantes de Carranza, and Alonso de Castillo Maldonado—ate enormous amounts of mesquite as they struggled to survive while traveling on foot through the deserts over a period of eight years.

Two centuries later, another traveler along some of the very same routes across the desert, Andrés Pérez de Ribas, called mesquite "the principal form of sustenance in its season." Often finding themselves close to starvation, such explorers learned to eat whatever their indigenous hosts offered them, from prickly pear fruit to deer hearts and tiny amaranth seeds.

The testimonies and plant uses that Cabeza de Vaca and colleagues recorded on their arrival in Mexico City provided the very first documentation of the diverse foods that nourished Native American populations on the western half of the North American continent. Moreover, the culinary commentaries of these true pilgrims took place some seventy years before the English arrived at Jamestown and more than eighty years before the so-called Pilgrims set foot on Plymouth Rock.

It is easy to glean from such early Spanish explorers that desert dwellers everywhere in the Americas relied heavily on dishes like *mezquitatol* and *mezquitamal*—atole "porridge" and tamale "cakes"—for their subsistence. From the countless accounts left by Spanish-speaking observers—Cabeza de Vaca, Estevanico, Perez de Ribas, Juan de Oñate, Pedro de Castañeda, Antonio de Espejo—we can conclude that mesquite was not some rarified side dish; it was the bona-fide breakfast of champions for many desert cultures in the New World.

And yet, some early European immigrants to the deserts did not take to eating mesquite at all. Perhaps the grumpiest and most disparaging about mesquite eating was Pedro Font, who in 1776 wrote this diatribe about the Pima Indian fondness for mesquite:

> Perhaps because they eat much *péchita,* which is the mesquite pod ground and made into an *atole* . . . when they are assembled together one perceives in them a very evil odor.

Not surprisingly, the Pima of this era reciprocally coined a term describing the disagreeable odor of missionaries and other Europeans who lacked mesquite in their diet. Now is that cool, or what?

From Big Bend to the Grand Canyon, there were so many accounts of mesquite pods being the principal harvests of indigenous foragers and farmers at the time of first European contact that it piqued the interest of archaeologists. The most perceptive among them began to assess their importance in the prehistoric record. On the basis of abundant evidence of mesquite remains from caves and pit houses, paleo-nutritionists like Vaughn Bryant confirmed that mesquite beans have been a staple for North Americans for far more generations than have cultivated maize or raised grass-fed beef. But most contemporary citizens of North America can hardly imagine that a wild food was more important than a domesticated livestock species or cultivated crop for all but the last four hundred years of human history here.

In fact, mesquite was the mainstay for most of those folks, not the appetizer or dessert. The first nine-tenths of all human generations that have lived in the Americas have been hunter-gatherers who relied more on wild resources such as mesquite than on cultivated crops or livestock. Only during the last century, as the daily use of mesquite began to wane, did ethnobotanists have to remind our citizenry that mesquite was the chief source of wild food, "the staple of life"—the main source of *both* complex carbohydrates and proteins sourced in the desert borderlands. If mesquite species with sweet, edible pods cover more than 1.6 million square miles of North American soil, that means that they were likely the nutritional mainstay for people in an area half the size of the contiguous United States. The native peoples of what we now call the desert borderlands—from the Californias to the Gulf Stream waters—relied upon mesquite foods prehistorically *and* historically for their sustenance.

My main-squeeze-of-a-tree was not only hot stuff, but *big stuff,* strutting around all the way from the Gulf of Mexico to the Gulf of California. You know, from sea to shining sea.

For those of us who are already infected with affection for mesquite, we will likely find a certain pleasure in the fact that this plant has forged long-lasting partnerships with human cultures over many millennia.

And that is why I had hoped to find something unusually significant in the deep history of the mesquite-human partnership —perhaps some clues about how we ourselves might sustain "wild but mutualistic relationships" with other species or individuals. It would be nice to have another model for enduring interactions with others rather than thinking that the Western notion of marriage—"holy wedlock until death do us part"—is the only model for permanent relationships that humans can enter into.

Let me put it this way. It seems that mesquites and humans have
had a range of consensual relationships over most of our time
together. Of course, you might just say that mesquite has been "used"
or at times "abused" by humans, and that's not much of a model for
other relationships. But mesquite has also used humankind for at
least ten millennia, to disperse its seeds, increase its density and
abundance, and protect or manage it in the habitats where it does
best. Peek beneath the covers and you might find true intimacy and
affection there, not just a relationship of reciprocal utility.

This mutualistic relationship is one that mesquitero Richard
Felger calls *para-domestication*. Okay, okay, that term really does
sound a bit geeky and a little restrictive, but let me flesh it out a bit.
That's a loose translation of a term of endearment that I believe
Richard once heard from some *gaucho* in the Monte or Chaco
regions of west-central Argentina, where the South American *Prosopis* species remain in intimate association with rural people until
this day. It implies that *algarrobas* or mesquites are camp-followers
that love to inhabit the somewhat disturbed ground that humans
and their livestock tend to provide, but they don't necessarily need
humans to disperse their seeds as crops like corn and wheat do.

But it just so happens that the *gaucho* cowboys and their stock
are as allegiant to *Prosopis*—its trees and their sweet pods—as it is to
them. As Robert Frost once said about liberation and constraint,
"You have freedom when you're [moving] easy in your harness."
When our actions are not choked off or stifled, but done with
appropriate restraint, we are truly free to be comfortable, creative,
loving, and responsible.

Others, like the late David Rindos, have used the term *incidental
domestication*—a concept akin to *para-domestication*—to speak to
those loose but innovative and intimate ecological interactions
between humans and food plants found in wild habitats. It is the
same notion that Michael Pollan stumbled on decades later, in crafting his *Botany of Desire*.

Whenever David and I discussed why some desert cultures
declined to become agriculturally dependent on just a few domesticated crops, I realized that his insights superbly explained the

relationships that emerged between desert dwellers and mesquite over the last ten thousand years of their coexistence. He could explain why mesquite did not become a fully domesticated culti-gen—a crop entirely dependent upon human agency—while an obscure grass named *teosinte* did. That measly wild cereal was trans-formed into maize, the most "codependent" and perhaps "parasitic" crop ever to emerge from the Americas. Even though mesquite was far more nutritionally important to prehistoric desert cultures than wild teosinte, its seeds did not proceed to other stages in domestica-tion the way the pebbly grains of that gangly grass did.

Rindos surmised that the incidental domestication of mesquite and other wild perennials was gradually accomplished by hunter-gatherers well before annual cereals became "the bread of life." This occurred as certain trees, shrubs, and vines with edible fruit became dynamically adapted to a certain modest level of human disturbance around campsites, fishing holes, or springs, while the foragers meta-bolically and behaviorally adapted to the nutritional benefits that several plants (including mesquite) had to offer.

As time went on, the distributions of these perennial plants became more and more influenced simply by humans dispersing their seeds or fruits. But something else occurred (or did not occur) with respect to mesquite. Richard Felger has pointed out to me that mesquite pods are one of the few legume fruits that do not dehisce and either drop or propel their seeds out from the tree for the purposes of dispersal. Most other legumes such as common beans, lima beans, jack beans, and cowpeas needed to undergo domestication simply to secure this trait for the purposes of extended cultivation.

In any case, prehistoric humans clearly had a knack for deposit-ing these propagules in what ecologists call "safe sites" for germination and recruitment. What this means is that the seeds often got embedded in a nitrogen- and moisture-rich "grow pack" of feces, placed in the shadows along a stream bank or up against a water-shedding boulder. But certain other animals also remained good dispersers, continuing to consume and disperse the mesquite propagules far and wide.

That's why mesquite never became fully domesticated as a culti-gen that developed an obligatory dependency on humans; it kept other options open. Foragers never completely managed their pro-ductivity or controlled their dispersal. Wildlife—from pack rats to peccaries to pronghorn—moved mesquite around well before cattle and cowboys arrived in the West to do the same.

When the first vegetation map was elaborated for the Jornada del Muerto near Las Cruces in Southern New Mexico around 1858, it revealed that honey mesquite trees were not equally distributed across the landscape. Instead, they clustered around certain springs, seeps, or fertile patches along floodplains that had long served as aboriginal settlements. When archaeologists visited these places where mesquite trees of tall stature and high density occurred, they inevitably found that the sites harbored abundant prehistoric evi-dence of both permanent settlements and seasonal camping over many decades and centuries.

It is tempting to suggest that the first wave of Native Americans reaching the deserts and subtropics took up the slack in shaping and disseminating mesquite once the megafauna went extinct. As Paul Martin suggested both to me and to Connie Barlow on different occasions, perhaps hunter-gatherers became proxies for the extinct wildlife by maintaining the directed dispersal of mesquite to certain kinds of habitats.

Of course, other explanations come to mind. Did the earliest Americans simply dwell in the mesquite groves that the megafauna had already established? Could other mesquite-loving wildlife be responsible for facilitating these oasislike patches of trees where humans eventually came to hunt game or harvest edible pods and other fruits? Did mesquite colonize the habitats that prehistoric peoples had cleared and managed for maize and beans and field houses *after* they had abandoned their fields and villages?

We may never know why there was such a nucleated distribu-tion of mesquite around prehistoric and early historic human settlements. But the relationship between mesquite-kind and humankind was maintained in something akin to marriage for millennia. Mesquite seeds felt no need to leave the "bed" made for them by human activity, and humans had no reason to reject mesquite's many, many gifts.

Then something began to shift—even *flip*—after the Gadsden Purchase and the American Civil War. The Apaches, Comanches, and other nomadic tribal populations that loved to set fires and move from hunting camp to hunting camp were either decimated or sedentarized.

Miners, ranchers, woodcutters, horses, and cattle came in and usurped the hunter-gatherers' places in the larger landscape. And curiously, mesquite populations did a backflip. That is, they began to spread along cattle trails and horse paths just as they had along the migratory corridors of giant bison herds and wild camel caravans. Their seeds established on the edges of cow pastures and goat pens until the trees themselves created fencerows that were more impenetrable than any barbed-wire fence.

As the miners cut massive amounts of ancient, canopy-forming mesquites for their smelters and cook fires, many small and scrubby mesquites popped up in their stead. The cutting down of arroyos and dropping of groundwater levels from overpumping did not help. The desert landscape was left with the terrestrial equivalent of a million trash fish and a few prized trophy catches in the midst of an overfished sea.

Cattle had become even better proxies or surrogates for the mesquite-dispersing megafauna than hunter-gatherers could ever be. Being better grazers than browsers, though, they diminished the grass cover and thereby reduced the fuel loads required to carry wildfires hot enough to knock back the scrubbier, low-statured mesquite saplings on the upland ranges. It became harder to find the few trees with the sweetest pods amidst a forest of mesquites that were no longer being culturally selected for edibility. As beef became king, the inhabitants of desert and semidesert regions began to think of mesquite less as a staple food and more as a source of kindling, fence posts, and beams for building *ramadas* and arbors.

Somehow the tree that had once spelled "live food" to desert dwellers became recast as dead wood. It became energy to burn or build or warm, but it was no longer nutrients and flavors to eat.

Mesquite was undergoing a makeover into a stackable, saleable commodity. Few of the remaining Native and Hispanic Americans thought of it as their staff of life. Fewer still did ceremonies under its canopies, or in the roundhouses made of its body. Mesquite had become merely combustible. To the many who were getting addicted to fossil fuel and fossil groundwater, even its use as a fuel wood was becoming expendable.

That fact in itself is rather remarkable, for mesquite has been the primary firewood used to cook food and warm bodies on cold winter nights in arid regions of the Americas for upward of ten millennia. Just how could a resource that was actually increasing in accessibility rather suddenly become obsolete in the eyes of the majority of the contemporary inhabitants in the North American deserts?

Mesquite barely ever gets on the screens of most modern residents of the Sun Belt, the post–World War II surburb that stretches from central Texas clear to the Los Angeles Basin, and from Las Vegas south to Laredo. By the way, the Sun Belt is also *the* region in North America with some of the highest rates of divorce between human beings, let alone between humans and trees. Between World War II and the beginning of the new millennium, the Sun Belt region has accommodated the largest mass migration and highest rates of family deterioration of any single area of the continent. And most of those newcomers to the Sun Belt cannot tell the difference between mesquite smoke and hickory smoke or mesquite kindling and oak kindling. As Tohono O'odham elder Clifford Pablo now laments,

> Sometimes our kids go off to school without knowing anything about our foods such as mesquite, so we are at a point in history when we have to re-educate them. Once they taste, they pretty much like it. They say mesquite tastes like caramel.

And once they like it, Clifford and others teach O'odham youth that eating mesquite can help prevent or control diabetes. He thinks they understand how important that part of their tradition can be for their future:

On the res, we see that a lot of our people are now obese and suffering from diabetes. A lot of the elders are going around in wheelchairs because they are having to deal with the consequences of not having enough native foods like mesquite to eat to take care of their diabetes.

Fortunately, there are still enough indigenous leaders and teachers like Clifford Pablo around in the desert that neither the mesquite nor the traditional knowledge of it will ever fully break away from their relationship with us. They are our anchors, of both nature and culture, the two threads of the real double helix . . . the odd couple in the divine dance.

As Ol' Paint and I circled back to head out of Texas, I felt a bit relieved to learn that I was not at all the first human person to have become so smitten, fascinated, nourished, and nurtured by mesquite trees. There are others who have also looked up to them as role models, as mediums, and as soul mates for decades. Their cultures upheld a notion of matrimony between plant life and people life that persisted for centuries, if not millennia.

That's why I call my true compañeros "los amigos del mezquite."

Or for short, let's just call them the Mesquiteers.

Whatever you wish to call them, they're my blood. My sap. They're as much my family as Laurus nobilis *is, as my own kith and kin. Together, in our gatherings for mutual support, we confess that we are dazzled in the presence of mesquite trees.*

CHAPTER TEN

Tending

In the weeks following my pilgrimage to Big Bend, I began to wonder whether I was better off (a) just becoming a mesquite tree; (b) periodically partnering with one at picnics, festivals, and dances; or (c) just enjoying the company of human individuals who were every bit as enamored with this tree as I was. Enamored. Enamorado. En amor. In love.

I guess that for the time being, I was willing "to play the field." It was so hard to decide what I wanted to be when I grew up and who I wanted to be with. And I was just not ready to be called Dances with Trees by my Native American bros.

Yes, I still had branches budding out of my shoulder blades, spikes of mesquite flowers pushing out of my ears and nose, and lots of nodules on my toes, but I remained in that limbo between fully feeling like a tree and fully being "the old me."

And so I tried to sleep it off, to postpone making the biggest decision of my life: To be a tree or not to be.

It's was about then that I awakened one day in Mexico, feeling a bit uneasy that my dilemma was still far from being fully resolved.

It was also unsettling because I was slowly waking up next to my sweetheart while there were loud noises emanating from outside our bedroom window. It was unsettling to suddenly hear someone outside our bedroom shouting out my name and ordering me to "get with it" well before the sun had come up.

Is that what it means "to be in relationship with a tree," or "to be in a family way with a forest"?

It occurred to me that I had not yet evolved very far into treedom; that I was still quite stuck with the daily dilemmas of being a human among other humans who, like me, often lacked the sturdiness to abstain from simple pleasures like a cup of joe or a bean burrito.

In this case, the four Torres sisters were on the back porch of our little adobe abode that lies within spitting distance of the shores of the Sea of Cortés. That particular summer day, Angelita Torres was calling out to me in the predawn twilight:

"Horny Toad, you lazy bones of a desert rat. Get up, get dressed, and make us some strong coffee. We're waiting for you or Laurus to make us some breakfast!"

Horny Toad, that's my nickname down there among the Seri. (Don't ask why.) I was slow to wake up that day in late June, due to having stayed up rather late, listening to all the dogs in the neighborhood auditioning for parts in a local theater production of *West Side Story*.

Two different gangs of dogs—one from the north side of the village and one from the south—met in the middle of Desemboque to try out their parts as members of the Jets and the Sharks. They barked, howled, and danced around one another for four hours, until one of our neighbors finally came out of her home to tell the dogs to knock it off.

Apparently, we weren't the only ones in the village who hadn't gotten much sleep the night before we were to go out together at 0-dark-thirty to harvest mesquite in the coolness of dawn.

That might have been why the four Torres sisters were unusually drowsy, crabby, and thirsty that June morning. It may also be why a half dozen other Grumpy Ol' Women had shown up in our yard by the time I had gotten my clothes on and boiled up some water for coffee.

By the time the coffee was ready, another four Seri Indians were trailing in to have coffee with us and wait for rides into the desert to gather both mesquite pods and the fruits of giant cacti. Laurus got in the driver's seat of her SUV and fit five of the women in the car with her. Their cactus fruit–collecting poles on the roof spanned the length of her Honda four-door. Our old friend Don Miguel Gris fit another four into his van. I fit two more friends in the cab of my pickup truck, and then three youth ran and jumped up into the truck bed, carrying with them more gathering baskets, buckets, and canteens.

As the light began to brighten the eastern horizon, we departed the Seri village of Desemboque for the giant cactus forests inland near the ancient *ranchería* known as Pozo Coyote or Coyote Well. It was there that several of the older women had already spotted the best gathering grounds for ripened mesquite pods and cactus fruit this season. It also happened to be where their ancestors had foraged for mesquite over the centuries, for there were bedrock mortar stones for grinding the pods into flour nearby.

With trails of dust streaming behind us like smoke, we fishtailed down the sandy track in pursuit of the most nutritionally important and delicious wild foods that the Seri could find during the midsummer drought and heat spell.

I kept on thinking to myself, "Why in hell do the best foods of the desert have to ripen when midday temperatures exceed 110 degrees Fahrenheit?"

When I began to whimper a little at the heat that was an imminent threat to our comfort and sanity, I remembered the ecological reason for why these desert plants "chose" this time of year to flower and fruit: They were selected to disperse their seeds just before the onset of the summer rains, so that any viable seeds that fell into a pocket of moist soil might have a fair shot at germinating and surviving. In short, the timing of the summer monsoons—not poor mortals like me—determined the harvesting schedule. I was just one more truck driver hauling the gang out on the Lost Highway to Mesquiteville that day.

That said, we the Sleepless Mesquiteers were lucky to receive a relatively cool and breezy morning for our first harvest day during the week of summer solstice. You know, relatively cool: It would be barely 100 degrees HOT by the time noon came around.

So when we piled out of the vehicles just to the east of Coyote Well, we were still in the shadows of the massive mesquite canopies of the Arroyo San Ignacio floodplain. Our shirts were still dry. Four hours from now, they would be sweat-stained and shredded by cactus thorns and mesquite spines. But for the moment, we were fresh and so was the fruit.

While I got the buckets and paint cans and plastic baskets and harvest poles out of the pickup bed, Laurus trailed behind a group of elderly women who were in hot pursuit of cactus fruit. I have to admit, they were drop-dead gorgeous—every one of them, including my wife, of course—in their brightly hued long dresses, their bandanas, and their blouses, not a single floral pattern matching with the one next to it, not a single outfit color coordinated. I'm sure that the brightness in the faces and dresses of those ladies could be seen from the satellites circling the earth that day.

While they went upslope from the floodplain to harvest the fruit of organ pipe, cardón, and saguaro—whichever was currently ripe at the time—I gathered a motley crew of youthful boys and young women together. They wore hand-me-down T-shirts, tight blue jeans torn at the knees, or denim skirts with all matter of embroidery sewn around the pockets and zippers. They were cool, at least for the time being.

We were the ones who would go after the straw-colored mesquite pods now ripe on the trees on the floodplain, which stretched out in front of our vehicles. My friend Manuel Monroy instructed the kids, some of them his nieces and nephews:

"Remember, let's gather only the ones that are ripe on the trees. Let's leave the ones that have already fallen to the ground, even though they may look just as good. We need to grind only the cleanest pods in the mill this afternoon if we are going to use them for your fiestas or sell them to strangers."

One of the long-haired young men in his late twenties looked at Manual and me like we were nuts.

"Wait a minute . . . when I did this with my grandmother when I was a kid, we gathered every ripe pod we could find, whether it was on the ground or not. She said that roasting them on the coals would get rid of any bugs or germs that might be on the fallen ones. We were hungry then. Beggers can't be choosers."

"I know, I know, I agree with you," I sighed. "But to get some of the mesquite flour from your village across the border, we have to put it through a laboratory test to see if even the smallest bit of it has been spoiled by some molds or germs.

"If you don't want to sell what you harvest and keep it apart from the rest, you can harvest them however you want. But the stuff we sell we have to test, so we might as well just take the best."

The young man shrugged and plugged in his ear buds to listen to Mexican hip-hop and metal on his iPhone: Aztlan, Santa Grifa, and such. He then disappeared into the canopy of a big mesquite, and with his younger sister helping him, he began to gather just the pods still on the trees.

All of us moved intuitively like a school of fish from patch to patch, as someone caught sight of trees with a greater yield of pods visible from afar. One person would abandon his previous gathering site and start in at another, and soon the rest would follow. Don Miguel Gris and I would occasionally move our vehicles closer to the group, so they could place their filled plastic bags or baskets in the vehicles, retrieving empty ones.

I would simply brush a handful of ripe pods the length of my hand, and let them fall off the branch into a gunny sack. When the gunny sack was full, I would go back to the car and dump them in a larger can or basket, then return to the same tree. When it was depleted of its pods, I would move to another, and then another, trying to stay on the shadier side of the trees, especially as the searing sun rose higher in the sky.

Inevitably, an older woman or man would scold me and their nephews and nieces.

"Look, you left the ripest ones back on that branch that was just above your head. Go back and get those before we lose track of where they are. They look perfect for eating . . ."

About the time we were beginning to wither from the heat, we spotted Laurus and the older women—Angelita, Amalia, Delores, and Anna—poking their poles into a pack rat midden under a mesquite at the edge of the floodplain. They had just returned from the cactus harvest and were now looking for pack rats to spear and eat like roasted guinea pigs might be eaten in South America. Their cactus gathering poles were now turned around with the pointed end slanted toward the ground, as if they were crowbars or harpoons.

Angelita used her pole like a crowbar to pry open a layer of cholla cactus joints and mesquite branches that formed the outer armor of the pack rat nest. Her sisters Delores and Anna were poised with their poles like harpoons, ready to strike any pack rat that bolted out of the midden. As Angelita removed the protective armor from the nest, no rat emerged, but her work revealed a cache of mesquite pods piled up inside the nest. Her sisters shouted with joy, for the rats had gathered as many pods as it would take them a half hour to gather themselves. They drew in closer to the midden, avoiding the prickly cactus joints, and gathered up the spoils.

"My grandmother used to eat the pods *and* the pack rats who collected them," she laughed darkly.

"Two meals for the price of one . . . "

As we left the gathering grounds by ten thirty that morning, I wondered if I should consider it to be a tended place. The women pruned back old branches that could get in their way. They robbed the caches of pack rats whose nests they located on mental maps that they carried with them from year to year.

They also kept others from cutting wood or otherwise damaging the bounty of their clan's gathering ground and even named one of their dogs for the site itself. It was part of their family's legacy, even if they only held and shared the rights to gather its food resources, rather than considering it legally owned property. And most moving for me was how the Torres sisters had welcomed Laurus, Don Miguel Gris, and me into their family of mesquiteros.

My plant-loving colleague from Nevada, Kay Fowler, calls such stewardship of wild food gathering grounds "plant wifery" to contrast it with "animal husbandry." The plants remained genetically wild, but they were definitely managed with a woman's touch. In Death Valley, Nevada, Kay found that her Timbisha Shoshone friends would trim the lower branches of mesquite trees to use as kindling. These women would also keep the area beneath the tree's canopy free of litter and the dung of wildlife or livestock. They, like the Seri, knew of particular stands of mesquite that typically grew larger, sweeter pods. They attributed the larger pods and higher yields to the benefits of their own work in the spirit of plant wifery.

There are tantalizing clues in the historic record that certain foragers would carry the seeds or seedlings of mesquite, cacti, and other food plants to other campsites they frequented to ensure access to the best-tasting selections. And in the eighteenth century, Jesuit missionary Miguel del Barco recorded that immigrants to the Baja California area of bitter mesquite brought sweeter mesquites from the Mexican mainland to grow for their own use as food:

> In Yaqui and other parts of that [mainland] coast, the seeds [of another mesquite] have a good flavor, and the people eat them. But in [Baja] California, they are all bitter, and that is why only the beasts eat them. But in Loreto and in one other mission some sweet-podded mesquites can now be found, for these were originally transported from the territory of the Yaquis, or at least from the coast [across the Gulf from us]. They were taken from there either as seed or when the seedlings were very small and established here in [Baja] California, and they have grown very well under these conditions. These sweeter transplants were made after the Conquest had already begun, because in the time before our arrival there was not a single mesquite here on the peninsula which was not exceedingly bitter.

That the conquest brought only sweetness to the Cochimi and Guaycura natives of Baja California seems like wishful thinking, if not revisionist history. But even today, there remain a good number of *mezquite dulce* trees surviving in many places outside of the natural range.

One of those places is in front of the mission of Loreto on the coast of central Baja California. Botanist Annetta Carter estimated that one of the trees was well over a century old when she first encountered and described it in the 1970s.

Of course, the traditional practices of plant wifery do not cease when we depart from the gathering grounds. We drove back to the shade of a few old salt cedar trees and unloaded the buckets and bags from our harvest. The older women sat in the cool sand and sorted through the pods, looking for the sweetest and best. They tossed the discolored and bruchid-infested ones away. In the old days, they then roasted the pods on a long bed of mesquite wood coals to evict any bruchid beetles hidden with them and to kill their eggs. Instead, we toasted them in a rotary chile roaster, ground them in a hammer mill, and then sifted the coarse, smoke-imbued meal through screens and colanders until it was free of debris, cracked seed coats, beetle bodies, and stems. We then sifted the meal once more until it was the consistency of a finer flour. We weighed the flour in plastic bags, slapped on a label, and paid the harvesters by the number of buckets of flour they had each produced from their harvest.

Some of the harvesters held back enough flour for a year's worth of use by their own family, while others felt they needed cash more than the product of this particular harvest.

A century ago, nearly every Indian household in the Sonoran Desert had a large basket full of mesquite flour mixed with water and stored as a hard-crusted dough in the sun, placed above the heights where pack rats or other rodents would climb into it. Some women made arrowweed baskets that were larger than their own bodies, then placed them on the roofs of their *jacales* or huts, where they filled them to the brim with mesquite flour. Whenever they needed some for a meal, they would send a youngster to climb up onto the roof and bring down enough to feed the family and its visitors that day.

I saw one such mesquite container being made by my friend the late Pima Indian elder Ruth Giff in the 1980s, perhaps just to prove that the traditional knowledge for weaving such gigantic baskets was still in currency. It did not make it up on a roof to be filled with mesquite flour, but it did make it into the displays of the Heard Museum. Ruth Giff has since passed on, and I am unsure whether anyone among her people still maintains the practice of that craft.

But they will. Someday. Again. The pull of mesquite is in their genes.

Some younger ones of "my former kind" have asked me whether the loss of such ancient, traditional skills for dealing with the "fruits" of trees actually matters anymore. They argue that Tupperware, paint buckets, and chest freezers have all but made such basketry obsolete. They contend that hydroponics has all but replaced our dependence upon food plants like mesquites that still need to grow in dirt.

While technological change is a fact of life, I am sure that the demise of the broader practice of "plant wifery" is a significant loss to any still-vibrant tribe and to humankind as a whole. I suspect that the disciplines of tending and tasting, storing and saving, and telling our stories orally have long-term survival value, even for those of us who do not live out in the boonies year-round.

And I, for one, have never met a tree that I've wanted to spend the rest of my life with simply through finding it on Tinder, OkCupid, eHarmony, Bumble, Elite Single, or Zoosk. I prefer them in the flesh and care less for the cyber-forests of our current society.

I may be old-fashioned, but I still maintain that you have to get up close and vegetal to stay in love with a tree.

CHAPTER ELEVEN

Shelter

I had begun to feel as if I were sitting here in limbo—half tree and half human—unsure of which way my life would ultimately go. I instinctively gravitated toward other individuals whose lives were also entwined in tree branches.

Nevertheless, I felt a bit trapped. The metamorphosis had already begun to take its course. I had this craving to drink rainwater and eat desert clays, just as a mesquite tree my age might do. But I also began to realize how much I was touched by the sweetest and most generous gestures of humankind, especially toward the creatures and trees who are our neighbors. I was having difficulty choosing between one way of life and the other.

I first came to the desert when I felt a political storm coming, one that threatened to tear at the very fabric of my nuclear family and our society at large. After I fled from some well-watered city, I faded away into the minimalist kind of shelter that any true desert offers. That's where I first learned to accept the warm embrace of its most iconic tree. Along the way, I learned that some desert dwellers are far closer to that tree than I might ever be. Like the Torres sisters, these other desert dwellers offered to share with me a broader sense of family. In their presence, I did not have to choose between being in love with humans and being in love with mesquites. We seemed to be of all one clan.

SHELTER

Other Mesquiteers have offered me similar comforts. And although it might at first sound contradictory, one of the first elders who opened my doors of perception to this broader sense of family was a woodcutter. In fact, he knew more about cutting wood without killing trees than anyone I ever met before or since. He became my role model.

When I was in my Terrible Twenties, I purchased my first chainsaw for cutting mesquite wood, in the hopes that I might become a *ramada* builder some day.

That is to say, my impetus for doing so was not so much for cutting mesquite trees down as it was for building their branches up all around me. I wanted to be able to select my own shelter-making materials so that I could write and sometimes sleep in a backyard shade structure. That is, I was intent on constructing what Spanish-speaking dwellers of the desert call *enramadas,* a term which somehow got shortened to *ramada* in borderland Spanglish. Hence, the origins of what American tourists call Ramada Inns, which typically have no *ramadas* of mesquite posts on their grounds and therefore offer no compelling reason for you to stay at their inns.

Several years before I cut my teeth on my own chainsaw, I had a rite of passage into the world of traditional *leñeros* and *ramada* builders, the humblest of *los amigos del mesquite.* I had the chance to apprentice myself to an elderly woodcutter and master *ramada* builder, whom I will call Remedio Cruz. The old man taught me how to use an ax properly, which included how to not kill a tree but prune it for future uses. For that lesson alone, I will be eternally grateful to Remedio.

I mention this only because some folks have suspected that I am such a treehugger that I would never dare to take an ax or saw to a mesquite. But if everyone cut mesquites the way Remedio did, trees would never disappear. They would simply resprout from their pruned-back form and continue growing. These days, we call it *sustainable harvesting.* But in the era when Remedio learned to be a *leñero*, people simply thought it was the prudent thing to do.

When I knew him as an old man, Remedio was widely heralded as the Ramada-Builder of Highest Regard among Hispanic-, Anglo- and Native American woodcutters alike. He had probably learned his technique for pruning or coppicing mesquite trees a half century earlier, from the oldest of his male kin on both sides of the border. Remedio himself was born just south of the Arizona border in Mexico. At that time, there wasn't even a single barbed-wire strand strung between two mesquite fence posts along the entire boundary line dividing the two countries.

Remedio was still a boy when he learned to gather dead mesquite branches from the desert floor that his grandmother could use for kindling. He and his cousins would disassemble flood-tumbled or drought-stricken trees and stack them into cords. For such work, they would employ stout iron-headed axes and two-man crosscut saws forged from 18-gauge steel. When Remedio turned sixteen, he was sent to the copper mines in Ajo, Arizona, to cut both ironwood and mesquite for their smelters, blast furnaces, forges, and fences. He did so in a way that he knew would keep the trees themselves alive, but I wonder if his crew bosses at Phelps-Dodge ever noticed that. They were good at thinking about extraction and reclamation, but not so well versed in concepts like regeneration and restoration.

By the time I met Remedio, he was pushing seventy. He was still cutting mesquite with his old iron ax that he carried over his shoulder like a lumberjack half his age.

"I got no use for them chainsaws my boys bring home. Them things are always breaking down," he told me flatly. "And you gotta buy diamond blades hard enough to cut both ironwood and mesquite. They ain't cheap. I can hardly afford a diamond for my wife, so why would I go and buy one to put on a greasy saw?"

He had worked for years cutting fence posts and corral logs for farmers and ranchers along the Rio Santa Cruz south of Tucson. One time he built a mesquite *retaque*, or stacked log corral, on a ranch near Tumacacori, Arizona. It required more than fifty cords of straight 6- to 7-foot logs to make a 50-yard square rodeo arena where ranch hands and drugstore cowboys would train horses for calf-roping and bulldogging. He knew how to size up a branching trunk so that it would offer a couple of sturdy fence posts without losing its canopy. He was also expert at selecting Y-shaped trunks for cutting so that their branching happened at the very same height. These served as perfect upright posts both for *ramadas* and for hoists used to skin, eviscerate, and butcher fresh-killed beeves.

Remedio was exceedingly picky about the length, girth, and taper of his fence posts. He was discerning in other ways he selected and harvested mesquite as well. He cut them during just one prime period all year, for fear of how quickly termites might ravage them if he cut them out of season.

"You gotta cut mesquite in the spring before it gets hot in June. It's best in late May. Not all the woodcutters agree with me on that, but when I go back and look at a post years later, that's what matters for keeping the termites from rotting them. If you cut them after the summer rains begin, when the sap from the roots has already run up in the trunk, all the bugs like to come and eat them, because they are full of sugar. You don't want the posts to have a lot of sugar or moisture, or these termites and worms and beetles will riddle them with holes."

That had already become the longest lecture I had ever received from Remedio, but he continued on from there:

"Cut them at the wrong time of year and they'll be no good. Go get them when they're in the right season and right moon if you want them to last forever. See that fence o'er there? We cut those fence posts with my bro'er-in-law right after he came back from World War II. Just look, still real good and straight. My bro'er-in-law's already gone, but that fence we did together, it's still standing."

He would cut posts and even firewood for neighbors, ranchers, and park rangers for their fences, picnic areas, and *ramadas*. One time when I stayed with Remedio and his wife, Molly, he woke me up at four in the morning on a day in late May. Remedio whispered that it was time to go for a walk to get some 9-foot-long mesquite posts. He had cut them a month earlier for a *ramada* he was building for their church. I quickly got dressed, pulled on my cowboy boots, and went into the kitchen. Molly gave each of us a burrito of leftover beans wrapped in a cold stiff wheat tortilla made the day before.

"Sorry we don't got no coffee brewing or no fresh tortillas," she whispered. "He says he wants to go out there and back before it gets hot when the sun comes up. He don't drink no water or coffee when he walks that far. Says it makes his stomach ache. But you take some along in case he don't have any water out there for you."

We set out well before the twilight began to settle on the eastern horizon. He knew the path like the back of his hand, even though his woodcutting site was at least a mile away, across a wide flood-plain of braided arroyos. He didn't follow any road; he just meandered down dusty cattle paths no more than 4 feet wide. In the dim light before dawn, the trail sometimes seemed obscured by brush and shadows in the bosque, but I could always see enough open space before my feet that I could have avoided rattlesnakes if there had been any. At most, I spotted a couple of cotton rats and one kangaroo rat hopping away.

In cool, heavy humid air that had settled down on the floodplain, the desert earth was fragrant with a dozen scents whose names escaped me, and it helped to capture the sounds rising up from the mesquite forest. White-winged doves were cooing, and a few male mocking-birds were competing for the best love song of the twilight hours. I tried to remember the name of what I now know as the cactus ferru-ginous pygmy owl; it roosted in a large mesquite and whistled out its monotonous toot. I asked Remedio if he knew which owl it was.

"I don't know what you call it in English. Some people say it's the Owl That Glows in the Dark. All I know is that it's the one my wife's family has always taken cactus wine out to on summer nights just before the rain making."

"Cactus wine for an owl?"

"Just a little in a bowl. You know, fermented from saguaro cactus fruits. The same the people drink to bring down the clouds for the rain making. But first, they gotta ask for the owl's permission."

To be sure, the mesquite bosque harbored a wealth of hidden lives.

When we arrived at Remedio's wood-harvesting site, all the trees around it initially appeared to be uncut, with no recent saw marks or ax blows. Then Remedio quietly pointed out where he had pruned sizable branches away from the tangle of multistemmed trunks. He directed me to where, a month before, he had hidden the last four 9-footers to dry, spread across a few gnarly logs that elevated the posts off the ground. They had perfectly shaped Ys at the top of them, so as to support the horizontal *vigas* that we would extend between them once we had sunk their trunks back into the ground.

"I put 'em back in that small clearing surrounded by bushes just in case, so no cowboy could come along on his horse or pickup and carry them away. The last four, two for me, two for you. I already carried the other ten. Here, I'll load you up first, then get my own."

Lucky I was in decent shape back then. I thought I'd sink into the sand when he balanced each of the two 9-footers across my shoulders.

"Just start walking slowly but keep on moving. You know, like them desert tortoises. If you begin to get tired, don't put them down, or we'll never get them back up. Just slow down a little bit. Now go ahead on this straight stretch. I'll load myself up and then I'll catch up with you, to lead you through the brushy part. You should be able to see okay all the way, 'cuz it's already getting to be light. That's why we gotta get back home before the sun beats down on us."

I put one work boot in front of the other and chanted a song he had taught me. My shoulder and neck muscles cramped and ached, but I kept going. He soon passed me, and as he heard me chant his work song, he began singing it, too. Whenever he got out of sight and I became confused about which way to go, I just listened for which way the song was going.

Once Remedio was back in my sight, I started to relax, even daydream. I imagined the *ramada* I hoped to build behind my house, but as soon as I did that I realized that mesquite trees themselves had become my shelter from the cold, a buffer from the heat and sun, a protected harbor and refuge from some predators. What I really wanted to build was an open-sided sanctuary for life like a mesquite tree offers its neighbors.

Where I come from such open-ended shelters are called *nurse plant guilds,* for the shady canopies of mesquites and ironwoods seem to nurse along so many of the most fragile lives associated with these parts. I wanted to do that, too.

When I came out of this reverie, we had arrived at Remedio's home. He helped me put down our four 9-footers. My shoulders sagged from the strain of the weight and my face and neck were drenched with sweat. I was thirsty. Fortunately, Molly met us with two cups of strong, sweet, black coffee.

"Looks like I got two lumberjacks to feed this morning."

I could see how amused Molly was that I had made it back with Remedio. She also seemed a bit dismayed by all the grime I had accumulated during the rain of mesquite sawdust let loose by the 9-foot logs.

"It looks like Remedio recruited you as his assistant *ramada* builder, but he stayed clean and you didn't. Why don't you go wash your hands and your face and neck and then come inside the kitchen? I got *huevos con chorizo* for the two of you in there. Or if it's already too warm in there, come on back behind the house and sit in the shade of the mesquite. It's breezy back there. I'll heat up some more tortillas on the *comal* out beneath that tree."

It was already time to get out of the sun. Under the mottled shade of the lacy canopy of an old mesquite, the air felt cool. Smoke wafted over from some mesquite kindling where Molly flipped giant flour tortillas on the *comal* set over a wood fire. When she brought the tortillas to us, they felt like steam-heated cloth napkins.

Remedio tore one of the plate-size tortillas into pieces and picked up dabs of the eggs and Mexican *chorizo* sausage with them. I spooned a heap of eggs and chorizo into mine, doused it in red chile sauce, wrapped it up, and held it like a fat cigar.

"We got a lot done so early in the day, huh?" I asked Remedio for confirmation.

He sat next to me on a wooden bench, looking out at the desert beyond his backyard. "Well, it's just getting started. Maybe it'll be good day for building a *ramada*. Not too hot."

"No, not too hot. Not yet, at least."

As the remaining sweat on my neck began to dry in the breeze, I took my first bite into Molly's tortilla. It was powdery on the surface, but warm and chewy in the middle. I closed my eyes and savored the fragrance of the sweet smoke of mesquite embedded in the wheat dough. A bit of chile sauce and watery eggs dripped down my chin.

I found myself sighing as if I had experienced some deep and ancient pleasure. I had tasted freshly grilled tortillas before, but none that tasted more like the rootedness of mesquite than they did of the fleeting presence of the short-lived grass we call wheat. It was a flavor I came to long for whenever I had to work away from the desert for several years.

It had become the true taste of home for me. I had once thought that deserts were too thorny for me to live my whole life in them. Now, I realized, I was stuck on them for good. And the desert accepted me either way, whether I chose to be a tree or be a man.

CHAPTER TWELVE

Range

I have occasionally wondered what kind of home I might have if I ran off and just took up with a mesquite tree or simply became one. But then I remember that the answer to that question is already evident all around me: a home on the range.

I, like many before me, have come to love being home on the range, even when that home seems slightly de-ranged. I've come to love sleeping under the shade of a lone mesquite amidst the pack rats and cholla cactus joints, as the mesquite seeds in the cowpies crackle in the campfire, emitting that unforgettable fragrance of manure and mesquite smoke that has filled the Western skies from time immemorial, which, according to some historians, began between 1492 and 1521.

It has been stated that in 1492 Cristóbal Colón began the ecological transformation of the Americas, a disastrous set of events, which some scholars call the Columbian Exchange, and which I affectionately refer to as the Great Colónoscopy of the Americas. In 1521, Criollo cattle and horses were taken off ships in the port of Veracruz, Mexico, presaging the later conquest of the Americas by White Castle burgers known as "sliders" and by horses' asses in the US Congress.

Nevertheless, some good has come out of all this mess. Many of us have made careers out of studying the desertification of the American landscape, and now, with accelerating climate change, the study of deserts and their critters has become America's most rapidly spreading "growth industry." It spreads with the speed of greenhouse gases and the growth rate of Bermuda grass on a hot summer day.

Why I so explicitly mention desertification—the impoverishment of vegetative cover in drought-vulnerable lands—is that in some people's minds, mesquite is seen to be culpable of perpetrating that heinous act. But I am here to stand witness that my partner mesquite has been wrongly accused of crimes against humanity and against our planet and therefore needs to be given a little more slack. For me, getting rid of mesquites on the range as if they are guilty of causing desertification would be like throwing my "babe" out with the bathwater.

And so, whenever I am able, I endeavor to go out and meet the ecological chaperones who guard mesquite's reputation, who know so much about the tree that they help me defend its integrity, keeping it untarnished and unvarnished.

Of course, that does not mean that such self-appointed chaperones are necessarily good at maintaining their own reputations; neither am I. One time, mesquite ecologist Ed Fredrickson and I both got dismissed from our roles as guest speakers at a career day at San Andres High School in Mesilla, New Mexico. When the hosting teacher asked us what in high school had most prepared us for our current careers, Ed looked at her and said:

"Sorry, ma'am, I'm not sure I should be answering that question. You see, I never finished high school. I was spending most of my time out in the woods back then."

I glanced over at Ed and grinned. He was poker-faced, but his eyes were smiling beneath his wire rims. Ed looked like a tall, lean cowboy, with a plaid Western-style snap-button shirt, Wrangler jeans, a sweat-stained felt cowboy hat, and dusty boots. But no one who has listened to him would ever take him for a country bumpkin. He's probably one of the two or three brightest and most capable scientists I have ever met.

"You never told me you were a high school dropout," I said. "So am I. If I hadn't played hooky so much from my freshman year on, I don't think I would have become a naturalist and, later on, a scientist. I stayed out in the sand dunes so much that I must have ended up with sand in my brain, not just in my ears. I never even got halfway through my junior year . . . "

The teacher feigned a cough.

"Well," she said, "let's change the subject. Do any students have questions for either of these scientists? If not, let's take a break and we can talk with them more informally, you know, one on one. Thank you for coming here today, *Dr.* Fredrickson and *Dr.* Nabhan."

Most of the students swarmed out into the hall, but one rather shy student came up to me as Ed was thanking the teacher for inviting us to the school.

"They say you live over near Tucson and, like, well, you even worked at that Desert Museum. When our class went on a field trip to Tucson to visit Biosphere 2 and the Desert Museum, most of my friends only liked it when we were in that big bubble at the Biosphere. They thought it was like a spaceship, but I was kinda bored by it, you know, by being inside. I really liked being with all those desert plants and animals around on the Desert Museum grounds a lot more. Say, how do you get a job at a place like that?"

"Well," I answered, "play hooky a lot. Ed and I are friends because we both sorta apprenticed ourselves to a bunch of mesquite trees rather than staying inside. We learned far more from them outside than from any high school or university teachers we had in classrooms. Just find a good mentor, like a mesquite tree, and learn all you can from that mentor, and then maybe something like a job will emerge out of that."

"Awesome. I go nuts staying all cooped up in front of some computer screen in a smelly room . . . "

Before I could say anything else, Ed tugged on my shirt and nodded toward the door. I quickly tipped my hat to the teacher and followed him out. We got into his pickup and lit out for the 197,000 acres of the Jornada Experimental Range where Ed worked. We were on our way to visit our mentors, to meet the mesquites.

The Jornada Range begins less than twenty miles north of the little western town of Las Cruces, New Mexico, but it covers roughly the same areal extent as New York City. They probably have about the same population sizes, but in New York, the inhabitants are mostly property developers and lawyers and such, while around Cruces, they're mostly coyotes and mesquites. The Jornada Range was established in 1912 as an experimental ground for learning how best to manage desert landscapes for the economic production of livestock and, coincidentally, for the reduction of mesquites.

But thanks to innovative scientists like Ed, the Jornada Range has become far more than that. It is the primary site in the Chihuahuan Desert for understanding patterns of change in mesquite-dominated grasslands. For years, Ed played a pivotal role in discerning those historic patterns of plants scattered along the *Jornada del Muerto*—the so-called "Trail of Death" leading from El Paso across the desert toward Albuquerque.

For an entire week in the early 1990s, Ed and I went out nearly every day to drive and hike in and around the Jornada Range. We spent hours each day looking at various experiments his predecessors had implemented to better understand the world dominated by mesquites. By the very way he patiently explained to me all the influences at work on the life of a mesquite tree, I realized that Ed had somehow taken on the "mind of a mesquite."

What I mean is that our time out on the range was like walking next to a talking tree and listening to its family's history. It was one of the greatest gifts anyone could have ever offered me, given how close I was to wanting to be fully transformed into a mesquite tree myself. That's because Ed not only had a certain brotherly affection for mesquites, but because he was such an astute observer of the nature of the desert as a whole. It seemed that he knew the history of the Jornada by chapter and verse, just as some people recite the Bible.

Following his arrival at the Jornada in 1987, Ed had taken on monitoring the long-term consequences of some of those historic experiments, discerning and freshly interpreting the patterns that emerged out of attempts to burn, graze, browse, rest, fertilize, or add moisture to various rangeland plots that were with or without mesquite cover.

For close to a quarter century, Ed tirelessly endeavored to gain a long view of what has happened to the mesquite, as well as to the wildlife and ranching communities it serves. He drew upon every possible perspective—from environmental archaeology and chemical ecology to chaos theory and resilience thinking—to make sense of the ebb and flow of mesquite populations. It was a bit like learning my own family's medical history from a country doctor who had been taking care of my family for multiple generations.

Sometimes when we were driving around in his pickup, Ed talked about mesquite as if it were a person—as if the tree itself was the wise sage of the desert.

"It is so doggone long-lived, so tenacious. Somehow mesquite has found a way to benefit from hardships that kill most other forms of life out here."

I perked up, hearing that bit of wisdom. Maybe becoming a mesquite might extend my own longevity.

What Ed offered me that week was a golden opportunity to deeply fathom not just a single species—mesquite—but its entire natural community as it dynamically responded to changes in climate, soil deposition, grazing, and fire cessation. Ironically, his "Rosetta Stone" of desert dynamics is what others have dismissed as merely "the mesquite problem."

In fact, some of his predecessors at Jornada were so obsessively set on halting the "shrub invasion" of mesquites onto grasslands, that they could not see the forest for the trees. They sought only to manage those lands for the optimal if not exclusive use of cattle.

You see, for a long time, mesquite and livestock seemed to be inextricably tied up with one another.

As cattle and horses increased on the range, so did mesquite in many places. Of course, each cowboy or Indian culture, each introduced livestock species, and each breed of cattle had a distinctive relationship to mesquite. For instance, it took many decades of contact with livestock before tribes like the Apache and O'odham began to intentionally corral and control herds of horses, cows, sheep, and goats between fenced pastures. Before the Civil War, the Apache and O'odham simply hunted livestock as if it were game. Where they overlapped with mesquite, that certainly affected the population densities of mesquites, shrubs, and grasses. But after the Civil War, "the Indian problem" became the main concern of the US military and tribes were sedentarized. Stocking rates of all European breeds of stock grew exponentially, and so did the "mesquite problem."

Neither Ed nor I particularly cottoned to the notion of Indians or mesquites being treated as mere "problems," and the changes on Western lands ushered in after the "control" of Native American populations began were sobering.

Even the most modest estimates we have of the proliferation of introduced breeds of livestock are staggering. In Texas, the livestock industry grew from half a million cattle, goats, and sheep in the 1830s to more than nine million stock of all kinds by 1900. In New Mexico, there were less than 160,000 cattle in 1870, but their herds of several breeds grew to include more than a million head in just sixteen years. That created a sort of nursery ground for mesquite seedlings.

Between the 1850s and the second Dust Bowl of the mid-1950s, mesquite increased its densities on fifty-six million acres of Texas grasslands, ten million acres of land in New Mexico, nine million acres of land in Arizona, and perhaps an area equal to these seventy-five million acres in adjacent Mexico.

Mesquite miller and woodworker Dave Perino once summed up the sweep of mesquite history on the range to me with a touch of irony:

> Ranchers in Texas have been eradicating mesquite for 65 years, *with serious money*—billions of dollars spent to eradicate it—and they now have 20 percent more mesquite today than they did 65 years ago.

Despite mesquite's well-documented antiquity in the Southwest, government agency pamphlets began to refer to mesquite as a weedy, worthless invader and even as an exotic. The writers of those government-sponsored circulars used virtually the same jargon that appeared in anti-immigration propaganda from the same era, propaganda that marginalized the Mexicans and even legally documented Mexican-Americans who came seeking "easy work" on the farms and ranches of the region.

But mesquite's distribution didn't really *expand* very much to reach its ninety-nine million–acre geographic range in the United States during this period. It just increased its density. In fact, from the 1850s to the 1950s, mesquite increased its densities across three-quarters of its distribution in the continental United States.

There is a sound reason to consider the Northern European breeds of cattle as the true "triggers of change" during that era, for unlike the Spanish-introduced Criollo breeds brought in three centuries earlier, the Herefords and the Angus had a propensity to graze grass rather than browse mesquite. After the 1880s, stocking rates with other Northern European breeds of stock grew exponentially, but the ones that were selected were ones that preferred to feed on grass more than browse.

Because it was thorny browse and not grass, ranchers began to treat mesquite as if it were "old and in the way." No matter how much folks like Ed and me tried to convince some ranchers that cattle needed some browse and seasonal feed in addition to grass, they could not hear this message. Our affection for mesquite did not translate.

But as Dan Janzen and Paul Martin had discovered, certain breeds (especially of horses) tend to spread germinable seeds better than others. Over the decades that Ed could track the effects of Northern European cattle breeds, the mesquites of the Jornada Range increased from 4.8 percent of the cover to 50.3 percent, while vegetative cover dominated by grasses declined from 90 percent to 25 percent. But even then, much of the mesquite increases were a response to lost soil profiles and grass cover, rather than cattle being the primary cause of either factor.

It was beginning to dawn on me that if I were to become a mesquite, I would have to keep adapting to both ecological and economic factors, as the context around me kept shifting and morphing. I would need to become the coyote of the plant world.

In retrospect, I can see today how much Ed's way of speaking and taking the long view of mesquite has held sway in the overall debate about mesquite in southwestern North America. After decades of speaking only of "invasions," "encroachment," and "the war on mesquite," range scientists now apply a completely different vocabulary to the many issues surrounding the waxing and waning of desert grasslands. Ed spoke of "chaotic complex systems" and "disturbance regimes." He is far more likely than his predecessors to see the range of roles that mesquite trees have played in responding to or even benefiting from changes on the range.

Ed had found a way to understand mesquite dynamics through many lenses, seeing the diverse ways that both natural and human-induced pressures change how mesquite grasslands develop over time. In Ed's world vision, people are embedded in that living community and do not stand outside it peering in. Ranchers are active participants in shaping mesquite's trajectories, rather than being either culprits or passive victims. Ed also worked with ranchers in both Mexico and the United States to propose pragmatic solutions to mesquite management that may ultimately benefit family ranch operations within mesquite-dominated landscapes.

Growing up in rural communities himself, Ed often reminds his peers in Ivory Towers of the fact that "people living close to the land are often in a position to most effectively manage the natural resources that support their livelihoods." Not many scientists of his era had the humility and graciousness to acknowledge that fact.

One of Ed's most fascinating insights has been that the nature of desert grasslands began to dramatically shift around 1850, at least for those landscapes where some mesquites were found within sight of the Organ Mountains. Rather suddenly, the rates of soil erosion began to increase in that desert landscape.

Perhaps it had to do with the end of "the little Ice Age" and the accelerated stocking of cattle on ranges that had been formerly inaccessible to ranchers because of the presence of Apaches there. But even where the wind deposited some of this newly eroded material, no strata of carbonates or other hardened sediments have formed there since that time.

In fact, most loose, fertile soil has been scoured away by the wind, with a greater loss of material than deposition. Grasses could not easily survive during drought years in such little soil, and the herds of cattle and goats that arrived ate most of the grass away during periods of stress. Fires became more infrequent. And with all the stress and disturbance in the system, mesquite had no trouble moving into new areas as cattle deposited their seeds in open sites.

To cut to the chase, mesquite was less the cause and more the embodied response of what has happened there. It is like the natural substances that herbalists and doctors now call *adaptogens*, ones that help the body adapt to stress and exert some calming effect upon bodily processes.

In this case, mesquite is the *adaptogen* for the body we call the desert grassland ecosystem. I wondered if I too could become such a changling, a shape shifter, a chimera . . . like coyotes, mesquites, and the Marfa lights of West Texas . . .

In short, the growth of honey mesquites is simply an essential part of a broader adaptive response of all vegetation found in desert regions to long-term changes in the surrounding habitat. But that's exactly why we should not think of throwing the "baby mesquites" out with the bathwater. They are *in dynamic relationship* there with other plants, soil microbes, and animals. While they are perhaps the most "vocal" messenger of changing relationships happening on the northern edges of the desert, we should not "kill the messenger" as if that might stop the message from being received.

After freshly analyzing long-term trends based on hundreds of previous studies, Ed and his colleagues have essentially proposed a new way of peering through mesquite's "looking glass." I'd say that they understand the very swings in relationships better than most marriage counselors do.

In going deeper and deeper into mesquite "consciousness," Ed came to realize that a sequence of historic shifts in mesquite density and distribution began well before the arrival of cows, cowboys, and cowpies. In fact, it was catalyzed by a series of cause-and-effect relationships that have transpired over a much longer time frame than the actual duration of the "marriage" between mesquite and domestic livestock.

Ed's curve ball to the scientific status quo is this: Mesquite's dominance on semiarid ranges may have ultimately begun *in the absence* of the kind of widespread livestock grazing that Westerners like Billy the Kid have witnessed over the last 150 years.

Whaaat? How? Why? Because cows, horses, and cowboys inadvertently removed most of the barriers that had formerly curbed mesquite expansion and densification—barriers generated by the way indigenous peoples formerly managed the same lands with fire.

Whoa, Kemosabe, where in the heck did that curve ball come from?

For range scientists, Ed's hypothesis has been treated as the ecological equivalent of Galileo asserting that the earth moves around the sun, rather than the sun moving around the earth. Just as the earth was no longer seen as the center of the universe, as was widely believed in Europe up until about four hundred years ago, mesquite itself can no longer be considered the *problem* we thought it was. Mesquite can be more appropriately viewed as an "indicator" or diagnostic "symptom" of a more pervasive problem, not its cause.

Do you see how turning the mesquite world upside down has implications for range managers whose former toolkits were largely equipped with bulldozers, steel chains, chainsaws, and herbicides? Poisoning or hacking away at mesquite will simply not arrest the ecological processes that have caused mesquite to increase, nor would it bring back grass, especially during a period of accelerating climate change.

In rather short order, Ed convinced most of his colleagues that mesquite was not the cause of desertification. This hardy legume had effectively adapted to changes in how desert habitats work, adaptations that allowed it to expand its niche after fundamental ecological processes had already shifted. Mesquite seemed to be like my favorite childhood hero—Gumby—who was able to stretch or squeeze himself into any setting or condition.

I was curious to see if Ed's sea change in the perception of mesquite had rippled out to affect range management in other regions and other research universities. I turned to a colleague in the Sonoran Desert who may be as observant and open-minded as Ed Fredrickson is. Over lunch together one day in Tucson, range scientist Steve Archer offered me an explanation for why most ranchers and range managers did not necessarily share the same insights that the likes of Ed and Steve himself had come upon.

"We as a society had been so intent on *killing mesquite*," he laughed. "For years, certain range managers had been trying to make mesquite savannas into something that had never really existed in the first place. They probably shouldn't have taken the concept of grassy, shrub-free pastures they had seen in areas of high rainfall and tried to force it to work in arid and semiarid areas.

"In all probability, the grasslands we have here in southern Arizona and adjacent New Mexico have always had some mesquite in their midst, but those mesquites were of low stature. They had been pruned back by fire or by people and wildlife. But when livestock came along in big numbers beginning in the 1850s, vegetation in the borderlands either lost the fuel loads it required to carry hot fires that dense grasses formerly provided, or the patterns of mesquite dispersal had somehow changed."

As Steve pointed out, the first shift in dispersal you can see on the earliest aerial photos of the Southwest is linear rows of mesquite establishing along the oldest known horse trails used for cattle drives across the Southwest. With increasing densities of cattle, mesquite jumped out of its old role as a minor player in some habitats to a dominant one in the same. If mesquite is anything, it is responsive to unprecedented opportunities. Steve Archer has contemplated this feature of mesquite ever since he left his family's home in the Dakotas to work on range issues in the arid Southwest:

"They are so widely dispersed by livestock. We've belatedly realized that it doesn't matter whether grasses have been reestablished on degraded rangelands or not; mesquite will persist there despite the apparent competition. That's because grasses do *not* competitively exclude mesquite seedling survival. The mesquite roots go down to lower levels so fast that they are quickly drawing on moisture and nutrients from strata below what most grasses draw upon.

"In that way, they are not really competing but coexisting. Cattle can even drop mesquite seeds in their manure in a patch of dense grass and the mesquite seeds can still germinate and produce seedlings that establish themselves among the grasses with little difficulty."

For reasons that I didn't want to have to explain to him, I asked Steve about the most cost-effective means that range managers had found for keeping mesquite growth in check. (I had begun to worry that the branchlets budding from my armpits and shoulder blades were beginning to restrict my movements.) Even though I didn't explicitly mention my personal dilemma to him, Steve laughed quietly for a moment and then grinned like a wise old Buddha.

"Even if you trim mesquite back all the way down to the ground in an attempt to reduce its cover, it has a virtually inexhaustible supply of meristematic tissue that will allow it to vegetatively propagate from the base."

Given my condition at the time, that was a bit disconcerting to hear, but what Steve noted next really made me pause.

"Gary, you probably know of that pioneer in fire ecology here in the West, Henry Wright. He demonstrated that even after building up as much fuel wood as he could possibly stack around a mesquite seedling and then burning it, it retained an almost infinite capacity to resprout after fire.

"So that inspired us to do a little experiment. In a greenhouse, we germinated some mesquite seeds and raised up a batch of mesquite seedlings. Then we began to simulate efforts to control them at the earliest possible stage of their lives as new trees. As soon as new seedlings were established and grew up beyond their primary leaves or hypocotyls, we'd clip them with pruning shears."

Steve laughed again.

"What we found is this: As long as we didn't clip below those first two leaves, we could clip and clip to our heart's content and these tiny little seedlings would still send up new shoots. We clipped every two weeks, and it just made them take the shape of a multistemmed shrub. They are remarkably hard to kill. Only when a really hot fire burns down into the crown and burrows into the root system do you get a real kill. And that's rare, even in the hottest range fire."

That may be why, as some sort of last resort, ranchers once turned to aerially spraying an extremely toxic herbicide, cryptically called 2,4,5-T, over extensive areas of mesquite thickets. These thickets had proven to be impenetrable by bulldozers with heavy chains running between them and impervious to controlled burns. It seems that 2,4,5-T did kill more of the mesquites than any other herbicide or extraction method, even if it never accomplished a 100 percent kill of the pesky trees.

Sadly, 2,4,5-T killed many more lives than its aerial applicators ever intended, because much of it contained an "impurity" called dioxin that can be toxic to certain plants and animals. In higher doses, some studies suggest that it may also be a mutagen or endocrine disrupter that can sublethally affect unborn animals still in the womb.

But might it affect unopened buds on a plant as well? I don't know for sure, because doing such studies is above my pay grade. But what I do know is this: How much we understand *or misunderstand* the lives of these plants matters very much, not just to the plants themselves, but also to critters like us. To spray or not to spray is no hypothetical question—no trivial pursuit—for lives will be taken and habitats ruined if we do not strike the right balance.

There are ranchers I know who have turned their own lives and ranches around once they decided to take such a question seriously. One of them is Ivan Aguirre, a Texas Tech–educated rancher in Sonora, Mexico. His day-to-day sense of striving for the right balance makes me both respect and love the work being done by him, his family, and his ranch crew.

Years ago Ivan inherited the management of Rancho La Inmaculada from his father, Maria Humberto Aguirre Romero. Ivan started managing the ranch at a relatively young age, and you might say that it has kept him young and open to the world, even though he now has a touch of gray invading his curly brown head of hair. Oddly, his historic ranch has a youthfulness to it as well, looking more like a piece of heaven on earth than the hellishly impoverished ranches that surround it.

Before Ivan took over the ranch, his father's work crews had waged war on the mesquite with every manner of weapon: chains, bulldozers, chemicals, fire, and other blunt tools. From the time of his family's purchase of Rancho La Inmaculada in 1975 until his father's death in the 1980s, there was always something being pulled out of the ground. Ivan later recalled:

"We had made the Sonoran Desert into an impoverished desert by our abuse of it. We eliminated the mesquite, lost the best soil, and therefore lost its moisture-holding capacity. At the time I inherited nine thousand hectares of this ranch, you could not see a mature tree left on the range." He laughs darkly and shakes his head.

"I am not kidding. You could look out across the range for three kilometers in any direction, and there was not a single tree to block your view of the mountains."

At that time, the mesquite on the ranch looked as if it had been knocked back and crippled enough to let grass grow in its stead. Ivan's father had instructed his cowboys to seed the range with buffelgrass, a controversial exotic from South Africa. When the buffelgrass seeding failed due to drought and other factors, Ivan stepped in to manage the ranch. He did so by following and amplifying the inspiration of Zimbabwean biologist Allan Savory, founder of the Holistic Resource Management (HRM) movement, which Ivan heard of in 1985. Ivan now runs HRM training programs in Mexico with Allan's blessings.

It has taken Ivan more than a decade to turn around his family's failing ranch enterprise, but he has done so by making friends with his father's old enemy. It is not too much of a stretch to claim that Ivan has initiated a peace and reconciliation campaign for the mesquite.

Ivan's efforts began at the ground level (or below it), where he first gained insight into how to restore the range:

> I realized that the mesquite's roots tap into the subsurface minerals and other nutrients that are rare in the topsoil of the desert. They are able to pump these nutrients into their leaves, which later fall on the ground, where they not only replenish the topsoil but also nurture the shorter-rooted plants like grasses with all this fertility. I actually wanted *more* of these desert legume trees—mesquite, palo verde, and ironwood—because they establish beneficial relationships with grasses. Mesquite, in particular, jump-starts the ecological succession processes that reestablish ground cover and rebuild symbiotic relationships.

Ivan began to use downed mesquite trunks and branches to slow water flows both on water-shedding slopes and deeply cut arroyos. He then encouraged his crews of cowboys to selectively prune mesquite trees where they had persisted, shaping them into protective canopies where wildlife could come to rest and feed. His wildlife populations increased in diversity and abundance, so he marketed the rights to hunt mule deer on his ranch for two weeks each year. Game hunting gradually became a major revenue stream for the ranch, which grew to eleven thousand acres as Ivan purchased adjacent run-down properties to reclaim. At peak productivity, Ivan ran a thousand head of Beefmaster cattle, while keeping much of the browse available for bighorn sheep, javelina, and mule deer. In drought years, he reduces herd size rather than placing more pressure on the habitats. But overall, he has dramatically increased carrying capacity.

From his perspective, a healthy herd of grass-fed Beefmasters is a tool—not an impediment—to the restoration of land health.

"The microbes in the manure of the animals that consume mesquite leaves and pods become the capital for regenerating the soil," he says, kneeling over a cowpie on one of our field trips. "Dung beetles and other insects also help with soil buildup under mesquites."

Pruning mesquites for better wildlife habitat has allowed Ivan to produce a steady flow of saleable products from the pruned wood for beautifully polished mesquite burl bowls and rustic furniture, as well as charcoal and biochar from the waste wood. He also found a way to piece mesquite wood scraps of various colors into lovely parquet floors, room dividers, cutting boards, tables, and doors.

Somewhere along the way, Ivan also became interested in Arizona-based efforts to reintroduce mesquite pod flour as a nutritionally rich food that can also help control adult-onset diabetes. Shifting his cowhands' seasonal workloads so that they could harvest pods and grind them into the flavorful flour, Ivan became the largest supplier of mesquite food products originating in Mexico.

While attending part of one of Ivan's recent HRM training courses, I realized that generating livestock, game, and five other revenue streams from mesquite was just one component of his holistic vision. By befriending mesquites, he had become a better steward of the land in ways that ultimately regenerated economic, ecological, social, and even spiritual rewards. But such rewards come only to those like Ivan who demonstrate the patience and passion to continue on with a vision of partnering rather than plundering mesquites.

"Part of our role here on this planet is to generate *riqueza*. How would you best say it in English? Richness? Abundance? Diversity? We are put here to observe the natural world and learn from its structure and its vigor."

Ivan's deep voice slides into softer tones, but his hand gestures become more emphatic and his eyebrows rise high upon his forehead.

"Much of the goods and services that society needs to survive ultimately come from ranches like this. Even though our society is increasingly urban, four-fifths of the lands in the state of Sonora still lie in the hands of stockmen. If we don't promote better means for ranching families to stay on the land—that is, if we don't revive a healthy kind of agrarianism—the new urbanism has little chance of surviving either."

Mesquite is no longer a problem for either Ivan or Ed to solve; they have made peace with their pod-producing friend rather than persisting in a war against this tree. For Ivan in particular, mesquite has become a means of creating health and wealth in a manner that has allowed him, his family, and his coworkers to live well in a stretch of desert long dismissed as being unremittingly hostile.

I had come to realize that I had as much to learn from some ranchers and range managers of the mesquital *as I did from the* mesquital *itself. They had seen the ebbs and flows in the ocean of mesquite from a vantage point different from my own. They paid attention to all the other residents there, from cattle and coyotes to dung beetles and deer. They too had a sense that we had all become part of the same extended family, the Legume Family of the Mesquital. I felt glad to know these other Human Beans.*

CHAPTER THIRTEEN

Ashes

As I ventured further into my quest to become a mesquite tree—or at least to become more mesquitelike—I realized that I had to let some old parts of me die, burn, become no more than ashes than dust.

I guess that sometimes we must bury—or at least cremate—who we ourselves have been, as well as the ones we have loved. We need to send those extinguished lives off to some other world in which they may be blessed in another manner—the world in which they feel fully embraced and comforted by this blessed earth.

And because of that irrefutable fact that human ashes turn to ashes and human dust turns to dust, I once took on a job to work at the far end of human existence, where I could see that process through to its conclusion.

Did I become an undertaker? Nope. A grave digger? Nope. A cremation kindler? Close, but no cigar. Not exactly.

The oddest calling of my life, hands down, was taking on the task of determining whether there were enough long mesquite logs for a community to be assured that their deceased elders could be cremated with dignity in their homeland. Cremation forestry, I called it.

My friend Peter Warren and I measured the amount of mesquite not in terms of cords gained from cutting down trees, but rather in how many funeral pyre equivalents could be sustainably harvested by coppicing rather than by completely cutting the trees down.

All the logs in the funeral pyres had to be at least 7 feet long.

"We can't risk having anyone's feet sticking out of the far end of the funeral pyre during the cremation," our boss explained. "It's traumatic for the family of the deceased. Make sure every single log is at least 8 inches longer than the height of our tallest tribal member."

Our jobs were contract work done on an invitation from the Tribal Museum associated with the four Colorado River Indian tribes (CRIT). They share a reservation along the river where it serves as the boundary between California and Arizona—between Parker to the north and Ehrenberg and Blythe to the south. The work came up rather quickly in response to a possible threat to a mesquite bosque on tribal lands that the Native Americans there were uneasy about.

The Bureau of Indian Affairs Land Operations department had recommended to the CRIT Tribal Council that they bulldoze their remaining riparian forests of mesquite, cottonwoods, and willows to prepare more arable land for rental to non-Indian farmers. A family member of the tribal governor had come back from his studies at Harvard just in time to hear of this moneymaking scheme. He remembered some wording about mesquite that his ancestors had worked into their 1865 treaty with the US government, a treaty that had also led to the establishment of their reservation.

In exchange for settling down in one place and participating in peaceful commerce, the tribes would be guaranteed in perpetuity the right to harvest mesquite wood to cremate every tribal member who wished to be honored in that manner, as their sacred traditions had instructed them to do.

To be sure, this indigenous student had a certain eloquence of his own, but whether his concern for trees was nurtured at home or learned at the university, I could not be sure: My sense was that he had a perfect balance of both influences.

"Aren't our mesquite forests worth more standing—in reserve for the needs of our future generations—than they are bulldozed away to simply rent our lands to outsiders? Our use of mesquite for cremations is written into our treaty rights. How quickly can you estimate all of its various values so that the tribal council can respond to the BIA's recommended plan?"

"What's the ideal date for you all to have our report in hand?" Peter asked.

"Can you get something to us by the end of the summer?"

I gulped. This stretch of the Colorado River—set halfway between Death Valley and the Pinacate lava fields just east of the Colorado River delta—suffers some of the hottest summer temperatures recorded anywhere in the United States. Midday temperatures of 110 to 118 degrees Farenheit are not uncommon on the reservation lands there.

What's more, we would have to begin our fieldwork almost immediately.

I began to worry about who might burn faster that summer—me, Peter, or a mesquite tree. But before I could say much of anything, I heard my colleague say:

"No problem."

I gulped. We had just committed ourselves to doing our mesquite fieldwork in the midst of the hottest period of the summer. I guess it would give me a chance to get to know a truly ancient closed-canopy mesquite bosque up close and personal.

The following Monday, a six-seater tribal plane picked us up at an airstrip outside of Tucson. In less than an hour, we had reached the Colorado River where it forms Arizona's border with California, and we landed on a small airstrip belonging to the tribes. Over the following forty-five minutes, we drove to an old oxbow meander on a segment of the floodplain that was so lush and humid, it could have been used in filming Humphrey Bogart in *The African Queen*.

Peter and I got our gear out of the vehicle and readied ourselves to do our funeral pyre counts. We based our unit of measurement on the average length of the logs we found in one stack at a wood yard near the airstrip and tribal headquarters, where families could retrieve the wood they needed for a ceremony to honor a deceased loved one. The logs averaged a little more than 7 feet long and were 8 to 10 inches in diameter.

We then walked into a junglelike thicket of mesquite within sight of the lazy river itself, expecting the worst.

According to the radio broadcast we heard in the little river town of Parker, the daytime temperatures would reach 104 degrees that day—that is, if you place unshakeable faith in weathermen. I have found their predictions to be wrong about as often as I have found myself wrong since becoming an adult . . . which is quite often. Nevertheless, the local weatherman had guessed right this time: By 11 a.m. ambient temperatures were above 100 degrees and probably hit 105 by 3 that afternoon.

But to Peter's pleasant surprise and my downright astonishment, it never got above 90 under the protective canopy of the mesquite bosque along the river. I mean *never.* The thicket had created its own buffered microclimate that was not anything like the parking lot that the Parker weatherman was reporting from.

Peter and I did most of our work in cool, dim light, for the mesquites' feathery leaves sheltered us from the heat nearly everywhere we walked. The work conditions were as comfortable as any I have ever experienced in my years of doing summer fieldwork in Arizona —no glaring sun, no insect bites, no sweat. The thermal buffer of 30- to 40-foot-tall mesquites was at least as good as what might be found in an old pecan grove along the Rio Grande or the Mississippi.

We had entered a true closed-canopy mesquite bosque, an altogether rare occurrence, for the sunlight hardly ever reached the ground after cascading through so many layers of feathery foliage. All of these trees had their feet down in the water table, so evaporative cooling made our walk under their cover rather enjoyable. I didn't sweat like a horse; I barely perspired as much as a beaded lizard beads.

The only challenge we faced was getting over or under the trunks of the mesquites. Some of them snaked along the ground like giant boa constrictors for 15 or 20 feet before turning upward at a 90-degree angle and raising their heads toward the cloudless sky.

I'd never seen such huge *horizontal* mesquite trunks before. Much later, I asked veteran mesquite furniture maker Stephen Paul whether he had ever encountered such mesquites and why they might have grown that way.

"I bet an occasional flood toppled a whole cohort of new mesquite saplings," Steve replied. "The mottled light could have angled their shoots toward openings in the canopy so that they grew sideways for a while . . . "

I think Steve was right, because water came raging across that portion of the Colorado's floodplain at least once a decade, toppling much of the standing vegetation, and then partially burying their trunks. The trees that hadn't been completely uprooted were given a new growth trajectory under the bigger ones. Only when they grew past the bigger trees' canopies did their growth tips shoot straight up toward the light.

That made the work Peter and I were doing rather easy. One of us could hold the end of a measuring tape at the trunk base, and the other could follow a horizontal trunk for 10, or 15, or 20 feet and crawl onto its enormous trunk to get the diameter at its biggest width. Whoever was at the trunk base would record.

Then we'd divide each set of total trunk and branch lengths into 7-foot sections and count stout 7-footers until we had enough to make a complete funeral pyre. Then on to the next one. The buzzing of honeybees and native bees was with us everywhere we walked.

Like less dense mesquite forests I had worked in elsewhere in south-central Arizona, these bosques were full of roosting doves, both white-winged and mourning doves, especially if there was standing water nearby. They were also rich in tree lizards and a subspecies of Arizona cotton rats only known from mesquite flats along the lower Colorado River from Parker downstream to Ehrenberg.

It looked like what a birdwatching buddy of ours calls "Lucy's Warbler Heaven," as if that little bird could not imagine a better place to mate anywhere in the world.

But as the canopy cover and areal extent of mesquite thickets have declined elsewhere in Arizona, they may have lost one of the rare mammals once considered unique to mesquite bosques— Merriam's mesquite mouse. The mesquite mouse was formerly common in the enormous bosques elsewhere along the Colorado, along the Santa Cruz south of Tucson, and further east, along the San Pedro River. In less than a century of groundwater overpumping, the drying up of springs and cienega wetlands eliminated the adjacent thickets that these mesquite mice required.

Once Peter and I had measured the mesquite biomass in several floodplain thickets, mapped the areas covered by these bosque habitats, and categorized them into three density types, we could finally estimate how many funeral pyres could be produced on a sustainable basis. That is, if no more mesquite habitat was lost to groundwater depletion or conversion to agricultural lands. Fortunately, it looked as though the Colorado River Indian tribes had more than enough wood to supply the next thirty years of cremations—given the tribes' current population dynamics.

But even if there was an unlimited supply of mesquite wood on the reservation, tribal lands kept under mesquite cover will probably be more valuable than the same lands converted to agriculture for leasing. For starters, the tribe was already receiving considerable revenue from beekeepers who parked their honeybee colonies in their bosques for part of the year before moving them to California almond orchards during almond tree flowering.

At that time, honeybees were in such demand for almond pollination that the California grove owners paid between $25 and $32 a hive to have two managed hives per acre delivered to their almonds. Many of those honeybee colonies did better if they had immediately come from a pesticide-free natural habitat, where the bees were healthy and well nourished, as they would be in the remaining bosques along the Colorado. The owners of these colonies would be offered top dollar by the almond growers.

After two decades of decline in honeybees across the continent, the rental price per hive in California's almond-growing regions had climbed to between $150 and $185 by 2012. In less than a quarter century, the value of honeybees—and therefore of healthy bee foraging habitat—has risen six-fold.

Try a little exercise that Peter and I attempted one time over lunch. Try to project the value of renting this mesquite habitat to honeybee keepers; the value of fees for providing access to dove hunters; the recreational value for birdwatchers; and the potential value of wood from selective cutting for tribal needs. They would provide far more income and social value than what you'd get from plowing them up to sow alfalfa for outsiders.

Besides, the BIA's proposal would have had the tribes pay for part of the costs for bulldozing the trees off the land; for removing all roots; for laser leveling the remaining soil; for putting in irrigation infrastructure; and for leasing the land out to whatever farmer came in as the highest bidder. It seems that the land would be far more valuable with the mesquite thicket left intact.

The last time Peter and I flew over to CRIT headquarters in Parker, it was to present a brief report confirming what most tribal council members had intuited. They declined to vote in favor of the BIA proposal to bulldoze their last great mesquite thicket. The spiritual and economic value of the bosque to them was just too great to mess up.

Remarkably, less than a decade after our completion of that work, the same tribal council voted to invest in other formerly degraded mesquite thickets and wetlands on their reservation. They contracted my old neighbor Fred Phillips to begin a larger, longer-term effort to restore mesquite bosques and wetlands in a tribal park along the Colorado River. With Fred's help, they christened this larger initiative "Restoring the Lost Forests of the Colorado." They are now working to transform the world one mesquite seedling at a time.

Fred began to build a team to do that work in late 1995, after preparing the Ahakhav Tribal Preserve Restoration Plan and obtaining the necessary compliance and land use permits to initiate a 300-acre restoration of mesquite, willows, and cottonwoods. His crew then designed and established a 500-acre wetland and aquatic restoration area that became accessible for viewing by boats passing the reservation lands on their way downriver.

Over the following five years, Fred's team helped the tribes obtain more than $5.7 million in grants for these restoration areas, including the development of a native plant nursery, park facilities, interpretive trails, environmental monitoring, and youth education programs. Their collaboration jump-started an environmental education program that has already served more than three thousand of the tribes' youth.

Since then, Fred has also helped restore 108 acres of mesquite habitat farther south along the river, near the Quechan Reservation at Yuma, painstakingly planting thousands of mesquite seedlings out on the floodplain.

All this strikes me as both ironic and redemptive—given that a decade earlier the BIA wanted to destroy all riverside mesquite habitats —that this collaborative initiative was later honored with the Outstanding Project of the Year award from the Bureau of Indian Affairs Woodlands Program, from the BIA's Phoenix Area Office.

Apparently, you *can* teach a doggedly conservative bureaucracy some new tricks.

But once the bureaucracy is tricked into supporting both native peoples and the plants they have depended upon for centuries, it seems that other stages of metamorphosis happen of their own accord.

What looks to be dead comes back to life. New habitats rise out of the ashes.

Once a life form as resilient as mesquite is given a second chance, it seems to bounce back—and continue bouncing—with minimal need for follow-up.

I've recently decided that when I die, I want to come back like that: perhaps not as a single mesquite, but as part of its thicket of relationships. I want to be one of those who resprout—again and again—to renew our world.

I am finally beginning to see the value of the entire mesquite community, as it goes through its cycles of living and dying.

I now see how different individuals, different cultures, different professions, and different faiths have either valued or devalued this particular tree for different reasons—for funeral pyres and ceremonies (spiritual needs); for honey, dove meat, mesquite pods, and gum (food and medicine); for furniture and building materials (shelter); for firewood (fuel); and for birdwatching and hunting (recreation).

MESQUITE

On some kind of planetary quiz show, I wonder how many contestants would be likely to figure out a single species with the capability to build around it an entire community of relationships that fully satisfy all five of these essential human needs.

Corn can't do all five. Neither can cows. Nor can canteloupes. Nor Oreo cookies.

The answer, I guess, is mesquite.

I can now love this tree whether it is dead or alive. Unto eternity. I guess I have finally passed over to the other side.

CHAPTER FOURTEEN

Shapes

I had begun to ask myself a peculiar question: not what love means, but how it comes to us. When someone claims that their chance encounter with a future partner was a moment of "love at first sight," what was the cue that led her or him into this romantic aha! moment?

Was it a purely physical, hedonistic, or aesthetic cue? The strength and suppleness of torso and limb or the overall shapeliness of the figure backlit by sunlight? Was it the fragrance of the prospective partner when one first caught a whiff of them (or of the bacterial colony settling in their armpits)? Or was it the buzzing of the birds and the bees around their heads that gave them that dizzy feeling of falling upward into the heavens above?

All of these factors have surely served as the sensory cues to plausibly passionate or pleasurable encounters.

But if you and I were to interview a thousand mesquite lovers, I would betcha that many would affirm that shape matters.

In fact, for us treehuggers, shape may matter more than size . . .

When I was still in my twenties, I met a bent-over old man who regularly ventured out into the desert to find certain appealing shapes of dead and dried-up pieces of mesquite wood. He brought them home to live with and cherish till his own death did them part.

They filled up a half acre of a "boneyard" that he kept way out in the desert, and they remained there for years after he died. When he passed away, none of his kin knew exactly what to do with his "found objects" of beauty, humor, and humility.

I use the ambiguous term "found objects" for his mesquite-based art forms because they did not fit into any easy category. *Found art?* Kinda, but he did occasionally hack at them with an ax or hatchet. For some, he would sand or polish them as much as any artisan, sculptor, or woodworker might do.

A few of his pieces could rightly be considered as furniture, if their three legs were cut to the same size and their flat tops had seats placed upon them. And yet, most of their legs were oddly slanted and the seats so small (compared to most sets of human buttocks) that most of his neighbors could not actually sit upon them without falling off. Others were like rocking ponies with four legs, but the legs were all different lengths. That meant that most of these wooden beasts rocked wildly when one tried to mount them; most bronc riders who hopped on them were ultimately bucked off.

Still others were sculptures or oversize "floral" arrangements. A few had the bases and burls of their trunks inverted so that the roots rose up like branches, and their pointed tips were punctuated with hard-shelled coyote gourds. The old artisan had drilled a hole in each gourd and then secured each one on the sharp end of a root, like so many beaded dreadlocks on a Rastafarian's head.

The old man's baptized name was José, but no one called him that or even recalled his full Christian name. Instead, his neighbors called him Mustang Man, for he lived an untamed existence. As his younger sister (then over ninety) once tried to explain to me in a stage whisper, he had long gone feral, like a wild horse. He had not slept inside her adobe house for decades. Instead, he rested under a rickety old *ramada* of mesquite branches any time of day or night that he required a rest, rain or shine. He rested there in sight of his shapely mesquite menagerie.

Mustang Man seldom spoke; I guess he let his art speak for him. He tolerated my presence because I would help him with the heavy lifting of his wooden objects, and sometimes I would remember to bring his sister beans or squashes for their suppers. But he would have none of the canned chile or soups his sister asked me to bring her.

Mustang Man steadfastly refused to swallow the White Man's medicines, even when a doctor had prescribed them and even when his sister insisted that he place the pills in his mouth at lunchtime each day. To appease her, he would pop them in the pouch of his cheek, but he would then spit them out an hour or two later after his sister had grown tired of watching over him.

Most of the time, Mustang Man sauntered along in the desert, simply searching for any curious, beautiful, amusing, or interesting shapes of dead wood left on the desert floor. Most of his finds came from floodplains where some windstorm, drought, or flood had uprooted a senescent tree from the ground and left its carcass for the scorching desert sun to fossilize.

Yet his love for these dead pieces of mesquite was not some rare form of arboreal necrophilia. Instead, I sense he felt he was a kind of midwife, bringing them into some second life so that they could be celebrated without the distractions of leaves, flowers, or shoots getting in the way.

Mustang Man often took with him a small handsaw with which to free the essential soul shape of the tree from the clutter of its lifeless canopy. He sometimes needed a hatchet as well, to loosen roots and haul the piece away on his back or in a wheelbarrow. He would carry it back to the yard behind his sister's adobe home and place it in an open area so that he could view the piece from all sides.

Mustang Man then spent hours upon hours chipping away at any extraneous matter, then polishing or painting what remained. In his later years, his sister's yard was so overrun by his menagerie that it became difficult to walk through it without bumping into one of its woody inhabitants.

"I guess all those pieces of mesquite are like his friends, pets, or compadres," his sister said to me with a deep sigh one afternoon.

"Well, I don't know what else to call them," she shrugged. "Once he feels he has recognized the spirit inside the wood, he has to invite it home to be with him. I don't know how to explain why he does it, except he never feels alone when he's around them. If I have to go away for a few days and leave him, I have this sense that he'll be okay without anyone else around besides those *mesquitelings*."

"*Mesquitelings*?" I asked.

"Well, after all these years, I haven't figured out anything better to call them. Just ask him if you want a better name for them."

"Well, I would," I replied, "but in all the years I've visited you here, I don't recall when your brother has ever actually spoke a full sentence to me," I paused for a second. "Even when I worked with him, I'm not sure either of us said a single word to one another. Come to think of it, I don't think I've ever heard him speak to you."

"Well, after ninety-some years of living together in the same place, I guess we don't need words. Sometimes I just forget that he doesn't talk to anyone anymore. I mean, I try to talk to him and I know he understands me, but he pretty much ignores anything I ask of him these days."

She shook her head and sighed.

"You know, he's more comfortable with all those mesquitelings scattered around the yard than he is with other people . . . or people, period. Anyway, I don't think you have to worry about whether or not he likes you. If he didn't, he'd run off to hide and sleep in the desert for a few days until he was sure that you had driven away. That's what he does with the government people or the bill collectors."

She brushed her hands together and stood up, then began to wobble away.

"Well, that's that! He probably figures that you are interested in his woodwork, or you wouldn't come around to be looking at it so much. He must assume that you too can see how each of them gots a spirit of its own, just like each of us does."

I couldn't say anything in response to that, so while Mustang Man's sister and I worked on cleaning and kneading her clay for pottery making, we remained silent for the rest of the day. Needless to say, so did the Mustang Man himself.

Up until the day he died, Mustang Man never spoke to me in words, only in wood. I would be working away with his sister, and it would seem as though I would hear a soft hum coming from him or one of his mesquitelings. When I would look up and glance over at him, it seemed that Mustang Man was fast asleep, or at least his eyes and his lips were closed tight. So where was the hum coming from? Maybe he was singing through the trees. Or maybe he was fully awake but as still as could be, so that he could listen intently to what the mesquite had to say.

After Mustang Man died of old age, his nieces and nephews rooted him in the ground at last, but I still felt his presence around his sister's yard.

The phantom limb syndrome, my shrink called it. As if I were still feeling a presence that was no longer physically there.

To my tastes, Mustang Man became the godfather or patron saint of all mesquite artisans, carvers, *santeros*, woodworkers, and furniture makers who have followed him on the face of this dry earth. The best of them, like him, learned to discern—or better, *divine*—the spirit in each piece of mesquite. Divining that essential character is a talent that I believe every artisan of mesquite worth his (or her) salt has as a God-given gift. Either you have that knack or you don't—it's that simple.

The notion that the grain in the wood of a tree tells you what to do with it is perhaps the oldest principle of wood crafting or sculpture. A stonemason will tell you the same, as will a ventriloquist. To be a good one, you must admit, to yourself at least, that you are no longer in charge, if in fact you ever were. You are in partnership, collaborating with the other-than-human world.

Once I asked Art Garcia, the coproprietor of Tumacacori Mesquite, about how his work as a fine mesquite wood artisan is different from other jobs he worked at in the past. His reply was simple:

"Well, with mesquite, I've learned that I won't ever be in full control of all the variables that matter; it's all in the hands of God . . . or Creation or Nature, whichever words you wish to use."

I encouraged Art to tell me more.

"I guess we try to incorporate Mother Nature's imperfections into something that is altogether distinctive, a one-on-one match. Those beautiful imperfections in mesquite are what we thrive upon, not uniformity or conformity. We're not looking to offer our customers a graded, pristine hardwood of the same shape, size, color, and texture every time. We want to give them something unique—with wings or checks or burls or hues that they can't get anywhere else."

As Art and I walked around his yard of air-dried mesquite slabs, trunks, stumps, and burls, I thought of the insight revealed to David George Haskell, author of *The Songs of Trees:*

This tree is taking the vibratory energy of its environment into its body. . . . Flexure of a tree brings within what was outside. Wood is an embodied conversation between plant life [and] shudder of ground.

Art Garcia then demonstrated to me why he thinks that the wood of velvet mesquite from the Sonoran Desert region surpasses that of all forty-one other mesquite species in the Americas:

"We've got us here a slow-growing, hardy desert survivor that generates a wood with higher density, a trait that is critical for stability . . . but over its long life span of a hundred-plus years in a climate with uncertain rainfall, the wood of velvet mesquite naturally develops so much more character. . . . No two slabs or boards are the same!"

I was dazzled by what he showed me: a long table with curvilinear edges that looks as if it emits its own light, as if it could glow in the dark. If Art had closed the doors to his workshop and turned off all incandescent bulbs, I think it could have done so.

Art also showed me a burl so knotty and gnarly that it looked like it had survived every skirmish, war, drought, fire, flood, plague, and outbreak of pestilence ever witnessed on this desert planet. Next, we looked over a beautifully polished curvilinear shepherd's staff or crosier custom-made for a Catholic bishop.

He then took me over to a tripod of thick branches that will be turned upside down to form a wild set of legs for an end table. It reminded me of the mesquitelings that Mustang Man kept around him. I asked Art about it.

"You know, all of this wild variability in shape and color is exactly why I remain an artisan of singular pieces, not a woodworker who can crank out dozens of the same shape and size. Nearly every time a big Internet marketing outfit calls me, wanting me to make a thousand identical cutting boards, crosses, or chairs, I have to stop them after the first sentence and tell them that they needn't continue because I am not interested."

"'What do you mean, you're not interested in a contract for thirty thousand cutting boards?' they ask me, as if no one else ever had the guts to turn them away.

"Nope. I cannot and do not want to give you thirty thousand units that are all the same size with the same shape of handle, with no resin or imperfections. Volume is not what I'm after. That's not what I do.

"You know, when I stumbled into all of this, I had zero experience in woodworking . . . but each kind of mesquite teaches you something. The mesquites from the river bottom of the Rio Santa Cruz have much more sapwood than those from the rocky upland slopes. And once I began to really look deeply at each fallen, drought-stricken, or uprooted tree, I could see in its wood the makings of a mantel or the legs of a table. . . .

"What I like about the wood of velvet mesquite is that it is a time capsule. You can see the history of the desert itself in each disk, each set of rings—thick ones from wet seasons, or thin ones from years when drought prevailed. . . .

"And the funny thing about this business—one that most environmentalists really don't get—is that I never go out to *intentionally cut down a live mesquite tree*, no matter how interesting it may look to me. Instead, *I rescue trees* that are going to be bulldozed, pushed into a pit, and burnt. Or I get a call from someone when they are about to clear ground to add another room on to their house . . . They ask if I can come and salvage a tree before the construction workers come and chain-saw it into tiny pieces.

"I constantly gotta remind people that mesquite does quite well regenerating on its own; it's resilient and it's not at all endangered. We just want to make the highest use out of the hidden value in already-felled trees that we can go and rescue."

Gabriel and José Escalante also find shapes inside mesquite trunks that they want to bring out into the world. They run a small *carpentería*—a makeshift sawmill and artisanal furniture-making workshop in Banámichi, Sonora. Maybe by calling it a *carpentería*, I'm implying that it's something fancy, but it's not. It is a helter-skelter workshop for guys who live and work close to the bone. Their boneyard is their backyard, strewn with all matter of mesquite debris, pulleys, saws, flap sanders, files, piles and piles of sawdust, wood shavings, beer cans, and sawed-off fragments of mesquite wood. If mesquite wood chips were edible, you'd need a hundred gallons of salsa to go with all the ones underfoot at the Escalante place.

If all that is just too messy for your taste, you can go inside with Gabriel's wife, and she'll show you photo albums of rustic furniture or swooping free-form bar counters that go for as much as $7,000. Their three showrooms are their living room, dining room, and kitchen, all in a modest adobe home that has likely stood on the Banámichi mesa overlooking the Río Sonora for at least a century.

Whenever I visit the Escalante workshop, I feel like I am arriving at a zoo filled with half-formed creatures. They remind me of the extinct megafauna that my teacher Paul Martin had me study when I was in school, except they're not at all frozen in the past. They seem ready to emerge, to *metamorphose* right out of the wood.

Once, I thought I caught a glimpse of a mesquite trunk shifting its weight from one leglike branch to another. It was like a nude model in a sketching class who stays in one position far too long and needs to stretch some tendons. Then she resumes her former position. I could have sworn that the mesquite torsos at the Escalantes' sweatshop were periodically moving in that same manner.

I once asked Gabriel if such enormous segments of mesquite trunks are now hard to come upon. He replies in crisp *Norteño* Spanish:

"Not really. We have no trouble finding large dead trees. Lightning-struck trees. Ones that have died of thirst after the aquifer dropped below their reach. By the time someone calls them to our attention, most have already died or have been bulldozed out by ranchers or road construction crews. We seldom have to venture out more than twenty-five miles to get what we need for a particular commissioned piece."

Gabriel shows me a recently retrieved rough-cut stump nearly 4 feet in diameter. It is an arboreal diamond in the rough. Next he brings up a pizza-size disk he had sawn off the trunk, then sanded, buffed, and polished to bring out its luster. I could glimpse the enormous swirls of lustrous color embedded in its rings: burnt siennas, mahogany browns, golden honeys, and purplish reds.

Gabriel then turns to me, holding the disk, and says just about the same line as Art Garcia has affirmed to me:

"We have no need to cut live trees. It's not efficient with the limited space we have, because a trunk of freshly cut wood from a live tree takes three or four years to dry down."

He gestured over to the junk piles behind me.

"With all this stuff, where are we gonna keep wood for four years before we can use it? We have a little more drying space at my uncle's place, but that is about it. If someone comes in with a big trunk of green wood they've harvested, we have to take it down to the other space."

With José's help, Gabriel fashions stools, straight-backed chairs, reclining armchairs, end tables, dinner tables, coffee tables, hat racks, gun racks, lamps, benches, and bar counters. His work yields lots and lots of sawdust.

Gabriel puts the disk of mesquite down and picks up a metal-pointed gouge. "Mesquite is fairly easy to carve because it doesn't have a pattern of grain that splits out like pine wood does sometimes. As long as you keep your tools sharp, it's okay. When we have a good piece of furniture with a little cracking or rotting at its surface, we gouge it out some and then put turquoise or tumbled chrysocolla chips in with a bit of glue, then wedge them in tight. Blues, greens, grays. People seem to like it, since it stabilizes the cracks. I don't get many pieces coming back to us for repair. This is furniture that can last a long time."

Mesquite furniture not only lasts a long time; it expresses its unique spirit over decades as well. Although its color and granular patterns subtly shift over the years, it's been favorably compared to cherry, ebony, oak, and walnut.

Gabriel agrees with Art Garcia that what gives mesquite its most unique and memorable qualities are its character flaws.

Since I happen to be a severely flawed character myself, I like that about this clan of mesquitelings. It somehow reminds me of Old and in the Way, the once great West Coast bluegrass band of Grateful Dead guitarist Jerry Garcia and his friends.

Wood from old gnarly trees (like me and Jerry) typically has ingrown bark in its dense, knotty burls, as well as mineral streaks, bug blemishes, and the impressions of latent bud designs. The heartwood of two mesquite trees is never the same. It turns through blondish yellow-browns, ashy gray-browns, reddish purples, and dark charcoals.

Mesquite wood technologist Ken Rogers claims that when the heartwood is exposed to ultraviolet light, it expresses a warm reddish brown, regardless of what color was exposed when it was originally cut.

I'm sure that's the reason why so many rock squirrels carry an ultraviolet light with them when they scramble around in the dark understory of a desert forest.

But I do know what Rogers is referring to. We have a rustic stool in our kitchen that came from the Escalante family in Banámichi. There is a surreal feel to its reddish brown seat, its honey-colored cross struts, and its two long blonde legs with enormous swirls and striations running up their flanks.

When it rocks, it sounds like a drum roll coming out of a bar band in a strip joint on the edge of some Godforsaken One-Horse Western town.

Although as many as 300 artisanal woodworkers in the United States regularly elaborate crafts, trinkets, furniture, doors, and floors from mesquite, these cottage industries do not have as much history in Arizona as they do in Texas. Fine furniture making from mesquite is an even more recent endeavor in our Dry Heat State, although our artisans are catching or even surpassing those based in Uvalde, Texas, and Aconchi, Sonora.

From what I can gather, the finer pieces of the mesquite wood artistry did not begin to emerge in Arizona until 1974. That's about the time I first saw the exquisite freeform desks of mesquite crafted by a rather wild hippie artist named Rory McCarthy. At first, he showcased his mind-blowing mesquite ensembles in Tucson, but today Rory is an internationally recognized interior designer and furniture maker in Sonoma, California. His past clients have included the likes of Pierre Cardin, John Denver, and IBM.

About the time that Rory sailed away from Arizona, Joseph Perino, a retired Air Force colonel-turned-home-builder-and-wood-fabricator, appeared among us. Perino talked a Cessna dealership at the Tucson Airport into letting him elaborate doors from mesquite he hoped to source from Mexico. When they accepted his proposal, he went down to a boatyard in Puerto Peñasco, Sonora, where shipbuilders were already making shrimp boats from huge slabs of mesquite. He bought some of those slabs and finished them into beautiful doors with push bars shaped like the airfoils of an airplane wing.

That makeshift, fly-by-night project launched the current mesquite woodworking industry in Arizona. Perino's doors can still be seen flying on their hinges at the Tucson airport some forty years after they were made.

Joseph Perino's son Dave ramped up the fine mesquite furniture industry another notch. Now the co-owner of San Pedro Mesquite Company, Dave used to help his father in construction and fabrication. He jumped into mesquite with both feet when a family friend allowed him to salvage the mesquite from rangelands on the Empirita Ranch between Benson on the San Pedro River and Tucson.

Dave rented some gift-shop space at Trail Dust Town, a Western movie set and steakhouse on the east side of Tucson, and began to sell bowls, cutting boards, and small tables. By 1976, he had set up a sawmill near the town of Cascabel farther down on the San Pedro, where mesquite still grew in abundance, unchained. In the early

1990s, Dave expanded his operations with a separate woodworking facility in Oracle, Arizona, where crews elaborated six different table designs from mesquite.

Dave and his wife, Kathryn, continued to morph their mesquite wood business after seeing how similar fine woodworking shops were utilizing mesquite in Argentina. Soon they were moving tens of thousands of square feet of mesquite flooring into high-end niche markets. Because of the gorgeous colors and size stability of their flooring, the demand for their products continued to grow at about 6 percent a month year after year. San Pedro Mesquite was soon grossing more than $1 million annually.

But for Kathryn and Dave Perino, it was not just about money or even art. They were fascinated by how useful mesquite was in other ways. They delved into mesquite pod milling after they learned how mesquite's nutritious flour could help control blood sugar and cholesterol. Soon they were getting more calls inquiring about their mesquite flour than about their furniture.

In an interview with Tucsonan Karen Gonzales a few years ago, Kathryn Perino offered a remarkable insight:

"Here's a tree you can't kill. It's too tenacious, and it produces a food—a seedpod—that's 20 to 30 percent protein, rich in lysine and other amino acids, high in fiber, [and it's got a type of complex carbohydrate] that regulates the human body's [blood sugar level] rather than spiking it. It grows without irrigation, without pesticides and fertilizers, [and its taste is] awesome. Who wouldn't get excited about it?"

When I met Stephen Paul, one of the finest mesquite woodworkers in the country, I was surprised to hear that he too was branching out. As we sat at one of his matchbook-style mesquite tables at his Arroyo Designs workshop in Tucson, its mirror-image patterns of grain dazzled me. The way he worked with mesquite wood was like baring the soul of an elder.

He hinted of a way of working with mesquite that reminded me of Mustang Man's modus operandi. And yet, he announced to me that he was ready to close down his entire woodworking operation to engage in another mesquite-related pursuit.

"So how is mesquite going to play into your life now, Stephen?"

"Through spirits."

"What?" I asked. "Or how?"

"Using mesquite instead of peat to smoke sprouted barley for malting into a scotchlike whiskey. We're calling it mesquite-smoked Whiskey del Bac. For as long as I've been in the desert, I've loved the smell of mesquite smoke. Ever since my wife, Elaine, and I moved downtown and began to live not far from where street fairs and festivals have mesquite-smoke grilling going on, we would have that fragrance of mesquite smoke waft down our way.

"Well, one afternoon, when we were drinking scotch around a little fire of mesquite chips, Elaine asked me, 'Honey, why couldn't someone make a scotch with barley smoked with mesquite chips instead of peat?'

"I took another sip from my scotch glass and said, 'Elaine, that's the craziest thing you've ever asked me. It can't legally be called scotch unless the barley malting is done with peat smoke; there is no acceptable substitute . . .'

"Well, the next morning when we woke up, the first thing I said to Elaine was, 'Honey, that is the most brilliant question you've ever asked me . . . Sure, we can use mesquite smoke in a whiskey, we just can't call it a scotch. In fact, your idea is so exciting that I want to phase out the mesquite furniture making and go into the malting and distilling of mesquite-smoked whiskey.'"

I bet that Elaine gasped when she heard that apology from her husband.

Since that moment, Steve and Elaine Paul's Hamilton Distillers has won more awards for their mesquite-smoked Whiskey del Bac than you can shake a mesquite stick at.

But when I asked Steve Paul how he decided that a mesquite-smoked whiskey could become economically viable, he simply said:

"I could sense it as soon as that fragrance of mesquite wood smoke reached across the street from the downtown festivals and entered our yard. Now *that's* what makes me and many others truly feel at home."

Oh, I too knew that feeling, and I bet you do, too. You just close your eyes and wait until you get a whiff of some sublime spirit. It is filling the air all around you and me, but we don't often notice it until we feel it in our nostrils and our lungs. But when we do, we must make the decision on a moment's notice to stay homeless or be homeward-bound, going wherever that spirit takes us.

CHAPTER FIFTEEN

Cures

I had now claimed that I would love mesquite unto eternity—through sickness and health—but what if it got old and tired of me, or I got old and tired of it? Would we end up going our separate ways? Could I stand to live once more without mesquite embracing me in my daily life? Would it become a loneliness too difficult to bear?

Well, I once knew an elderly woman who claimed that mesquite itself could cure loneliness. Her contention was based on the notion that black mesquite pitch could cut the loneliness felt by some elderly ladies who had grayed with the advance of age. They felt dismissed or marginalized because of that single fact. As she herself felt now and then . . . for instance.

Marquita was fond of dyeing her hair with slightly melted black mesquite pitch, hoping it would help her attract more dancing partners. Ever since she was a girl living way out in the desert, Marquita loved to come into town to dance. She simply loved to party. But by age seventy-two—three times my age at the time I met her—she was quickly running out of potential partners of her own generation. And so, she had resorted to regularly applying the jet-black gum oozing from wounded mesquite trunks to give her hair a brilliant sheen and ebony color. She refused to allow herself to be ignored or overlooked by the younger males who frequented dance-halls at all-night parties.

I had accidentally come upon Marquita at the B-29 bar in South Tucson, where I was waiting to pick up a Native American friend who wanted to see some of his cousins out at an all-night chicken scratch dance on a reservation nearby. His car was in the shop, so we had decided to go out there in mine and stay "just a couple hours."

When he arrived and joined me at the B-29, we ordered a beer that we decided to split between us so that we would have no trouble driving out to the fiesta. We were debating the exact location of where the dance was to be held when this black-haired woman in a red cotton dress came up to us.

"I heard you talking. I know exactly where that place is, where the chicken scratch dance is to be. I'm not only a good dancer, I'm a good guide and I need a ride. I can get you there if you take me along. By the way, my name is Marquita. What's yours?"

No wallflower, this Marquita. But about then, my friend kicked me under the table. Haltingly, he spoke up.

"Well, ma'am, I wish we could, but we only have a small pickup truck with two bucket seats, and my Yori friend here has the pickup truck bed all filled up with farm tools. I'm sorry we can't be of more help," he apologized.

Marquita shrugged off my friend's retort, and turned to me.

"Well, if you're the driver and pickup owner, why don't you decide? I could keep you awake on the way out there and back, telling you stories while I sit on his lap."

She nodded her chin toward my friend. He looked more and more alarmed by the moment. My friend decided to offer more excuses as to why her solution would simply not work.

"Thanks for the suggestion, lady, but it's a long haul out there on dirt roads so it would be way too uncomfortable to do that—have someone in my lap—even if it was my own girlfriend. And besides I've recently had a knee operation. It still hurts when there's any pressure or weight on my leg."

She glared at him, disappointed, then walked away, dejected. And then, she instantly disappeared.

When we finished our shared bottle of beer, we went out to my pickup, where I unlocked the doors to let us in. That's when I noticed a suspicious lump under the blue tarp that I kept in the bed, right behind the rear window of the cab.

"Marquita, is that you?" I asked.

"How did you know? Did you change your mind?"

"I saw some of your shiny black hair sticking out from the tarp when I looked back through the cab window."

"Yeah, that's my new hairdo. I got it gratis from a mesquite tree in my yard. It fights loneliness."

"WHAT DOES?"

"The black mesquite pitch."

"HOW?"

"By making me look younger so I get more invitations to dance."

My friend and I looked at one another. He winked.

"Tell you what," my friend said. "I'll ride in the back, but only on the way out there. You ride in the cab with Gary, but once we get to the chicken scratch dance, you are on your own. No ride back. Okay?"

"Sure," she replied, delighted. "By that time, I should have got me my own dancing partner who'll be willing to take me back home."

My friend got out and politely helped Marquita step down from the truck bed, then he hopped up into it and sat with his back to the cab. Marquita got in next to me.

I turned the key, backed out of my parking space, and then waved to my friend back in the truck bed. Fortunately, for his sake, it was a warm and rather windless night. I shifted gears, popping the clutch, and we were off into the desert to do some dancing.

For the next twenty minutes, Marquita told me all about how she prepared the mesquite pitch as a hair dye and how she used different products of mesquite for a dozen other cures as well. She was not one of those *curanderas,* she emphatically explained. But she didn't need to become one, for just about every woman from her village already kept mesquite products in their family's medicine cabinet.

I listened up. What else could I do? I was a captive audience for this highly charismatic motivational speaker and mesquite medicine promoter.

As minutes, then hours, passed while we searched for the chicken scratch dance, which had moved inexplicably from one village to another on a farther reservation, Marquita loaded my brain down with medicinal lore about mesquite. I took most of it in at the time, but as I try to recall every usage she mentioned a quarter century later, I'm certain that I only remember the barest details.

Oddly, the most vivid moments of our conversation were not just about her own people's use of mesquite, but of a vast pharmacopoeia shared with other Indian, Hispanic, Chinese, and Anglo dwellers over the last several decades. Her time in boarding schools, border towns, and military bases had made her knowledge of mesquite rather multicultural.

In the old days, whenever a desert dweller was bitten by red ants, he or she chewed the little green leaves of mesquite and made a poultice of the masticated mass to put on the bite in order to stop its throbbing. When she had a headache from working too hard in the sun, she soaked a handful of mesquite leaves in cold water and drank the resulting infusion the way a dorm mom at her boarding school had instructed her to do.

Her own grandmother used to make a powder of mesquite roots to apply directly to sores on her feet or knees or soaked the powder in water, which she then used as a wash for cuts, wounds, rashes, and other skin irritations. Grandma claimed that she learned it from a Chinese railroad worker.

Mesquite root powder could alleviate pink eye and remove dust from your eyes as well. She could not remember the dosage but knew that her grandmother also used the roots for reducing women's "monthly discomfort." Some people she knew also used the roots to stop diarrhea, although she admitted that other herbs more frequently sufficed for that task.

But that was not all. The "beans" were good medicine as well. A paste made from mesquite bean meal and cold water worked as a plaster to reduce the severity of sunburns. Other people, she said, soaked the beans in warm water and then poured some of the resulting liquor into the ear to relieve earaches. She had even heard of a man who cured his grandson's earaches by sticking a small pod into the child's ear, but she had not seen it done herself.

Still, she said, the gums of the mesquite were the best medicines. The opaque colored gum—not the black pitch—could be used to prevent infection around a newborn baby's healing navel. You could chew or hold it in your cheek if you needed to relieve tooth and gum pain. It was mashed and softened, then placed on chapped lips, cracked fingers and heels, or mouth sores. She herself had often used it on hand burns after she had accidentally touched a frying pan or grill when it was red hot.

The black pitch was not merely a hair dye and "dancing partner attractant," but a cure for other ills. It too could be used as a wash for sore eyes or as a salve for burns and foot sores. It served as a lotion applied to the privates of men who had contracted bad diseases like gonorrhea. Placing a poultice of it on pustules could relieve their itching and oozing. When some cowboys got injured away from their ranch headquarters or chuck wagons, they would immediately use it as an antibiotic salve. It could help to close and heal any major cuts or wounds suffered when cattle horns badly gouged a bull rider at a rodeo.

Finally, Marquita noted, as we reached the chicken scratch dance arena, the inner bark of mesquite can be used as an emetic . . . in case you've drunk too much alcohol or eaten some food that had spoiled out on a table during a hot summer night.

"But I'm not gonna drink nothing nor eat nothin' tonight, so I won't need it. I'm just here to dance the two-step and the polka and the schottische."

Marquita ceremoniously got out of the cab, slicked down her hair and her long skirt, and off she went. Within minutes, a handsome old cowboy recognized her, offered her his hand, and around the maypole they circled, two-stepping their way into the night. I was tired and thirsty and went looking for a drink of water.

When I returned to the dancing arena, Marquita was nowhere to be seen. Neither was the dapper elder who had offered her his hand for that last dance. I asked around, but no one I spoke with knew where either—or both—of them had gone.

From that time on, I have never been skeptical that a mesquite can cure loneliness.

Its healing spirit will accompany me, wherever I go.

CHAPTER SIXTEEN

Tortillas

If my relationship with mesquite has changed me in any way, it has opened me up to more of the good, the grace, the hope, and the beauty in the humans who gravitate to mesquites, other trees, or critters, treating them as beloved ones. They have opened my eyes, my mouth, my mind, and my heart to lives I had neglected to taste or see earlier in my checkered career—that is, before I too became a Mesquiteer.

And since then, one of the most beautiful sights I've ever witnessed is that of a woman's hands gently kneading dough that had risen out of a bowl of mesquite dough. Those hands belong to a woman that I hardly know very well, but one whom I know to love mesquite as much as the rest of us Mesquiteers do . . . such as Laurus . . . and Marquita . . . and Remedio, Ed, and Ivan . . . as well as the Torres sisters . . . and many other newfound friends and mentors.

For me, the way this exemplary woman moves through this world is concrete evidence that mesquite can change the destiny of each of us if we let it into our lives.

This mesquite-loving friend of mine has the euphonious name of Esperanza. For me, she embodies a kind of patient hope that we all need in our lives. It is the hope that each of us will be touched by the gifts and incarnate grace of some tree, be it a mesquite or some other species of strong heart (wood).

Sometimes when I drop in on Esperanza to say hi to her and her father, Javier, she seems to be coated in a light sheen of fragrant mesquite dust. I quickly notice whether Esperanza's soft but powerful palms have been patting out another dough ball of mesquite meal and amaranth flour into a pliable patty and that patty into a circular disk. Her nimble fingers, dusted with mesquite meal, stretch the edges and spin the disk until it is ready to whirl onto the *comal* and bake until it "turns to gold." Esperanza's fingertips deftly lift the lip of tortilla from the red-hot *comal* and fling it atop a stack of other disks cooling on a white cotton towel.

Thoughtful, determined, and infinitely capable, Esperanza and her family are living testaments to the power of mesquite to alter and better our lives. But that can happen only when we open ourselves up to species other than our own.

I met Esperanza years before on a street corner in Avra Valley, on the mesquite-studded plains west of Tucson. It was a street corner where street corners barely exist, for there are no traffic lights, stop signs, or curbs. The roads are mostly hard-packed clay in that part of the Avra, wide *terracerias* pocked with lots of potholes.

Esperanza was selling her mother's wares—delicious Sonoran-style wheat tortillas by the dozen. When her father, Javier, was plagued with cancer and its interminable treatments, Esperanza took over making the rounds that he once undertook each afternoon. Sometimes Javier would come in the car with her on these tortilla-marketing expeditions, merely to get out of his sick bed and to re-engage with customers he obviously knew and loved. While keeping an eye on her father, Esperanza hawked the homemade tortillas to passersby, but with an air of professionalism that could stop you in your tracks. She did not wave you down or plead with you, but something about her confident stance pulled you into her sales area on the side of the road.

Esperanza was in her early to mid-thirties by that time, I guessed. I quickly recognized this determination, confidence, and brightness about her, as she spoke to me in both Spanish and English with equal proficiency. She exuded a certain vivacious quality whenever she interacted with her rural neighbors. Neighbors like me—whom she didn't really know from Adam back then—were so warmly welcomed by Esperanza that I immediately felt a kinship with her.

I was in my earliest stages of trying to be a locavore back then, even though the word itself was not yet coined. Whenever I wasn't gardening, foraging, or quail hunting, I was out on the prowl, trying to figure out what my neighbors grew or made that fell inside the so-called foodshed of my community.

Javier and Esperanza were just the kind of neighbors you would want to banter and barter with on any day of the year. And yet, it must have been trying—being out on a street corner in the summer —hawking tortillas. Folks drove by without even cracking open a window in their air-conditioned SUVs. On the worst of days, more wheat tortillas than dollars went back home to their Camino Lucido residence in the evening.

Nevertheless, she was out there for good reasons. She had recently been laid off from her office job in Tucson. Her father's physical health was iffy, given the cancer he had been fighting. Her mother needed help vending her wheat flour tortillas. And they needed something more distinctive to fuel their fledgling business.

One particular evening, after having freshly ground some mesquite meal with Seri Indian friends on the coast of Sonora the previous week, I spotted Esperanza standing by her car. I asked if she or her mother would consider making me some tortillas from mesquite meal.

"From the *pechita* around here?" she asked uncomfortably, as if I were suggesting that she go out and forage mesquite pods each day on top of everything else she was trying to do.

"No, no. I'll give you some mesquite meal each time we meet, and the next time I see you, you give me some mesquite tortillas. You don't need to pay for the mesquite meal, and I'll pay you the same per dozen as I would for your wheat tortillas."

"Well," she said hesitantly, "we'll give it a try, but I can't promise you anything."

I gave Esperanza a 5-pound bag of mesquite meal and my telephone number. For a moment I thought it might be the last time I saw her. Her family makes some of the best wheat flour tortillas in the world. Why would they want to change to a flour that hardly anyone in Tucson had tasted? I worried that I'd been too presumptuous and had even insulted her.

A week or so later, I received a call.

"Gary, I have them ready for you to try. I think they're *delicious.* Well, you come and see for yourself."

"See what?" I asked, just as I realized that it was Esperanza on the line.

"The tortillas! I've made some pretty good mesquite tortillas!"

I flew as fast as I could in my pickup truck down to Ajo Way, our street corner rendezvous. Esperanza was already there, her hair glowing in the late afternoon sunlight, her face beaming. She opened a white cotton towel. Inside were gorgeous golden tortillas, still warm to the touch. She had finished the batch within the hour.

"Well, go 'head and try one. They're all for you."

I took one from her hands and took a bite. Its flavor was unlike that of any tortilla I've ever eaten. A warm, rich cinnamon fragrance rose from them, and their texture was as fine as her mother's wheat tortillas.

"They're fabulous!" I exclaimed.

"I know, I know," she said, and laughed. "I've never had tortillas with such a sweet flavor."

"How long did it take you to perfect them?"

"Oh, you don't want to know. First they came out brittle as cardboard, so I kept on switching the mixture of flours, and then the kinds of oil, until I got it right. These have olive oil in them. I mean, I think I got it right—I may have some more experimenting to do. What do you think?"

"I think I need to pay you more for all your time and bring you some more mesquite meal."

I bought Esperanza's tortillas for another nine months before I moved away from the neighborhood. Her tortillas became even better, and so did her business skills. When I told her that mesquite was one of the healthiest foods that folks suffering from diabetes could eat, she took a batch to the health food store nearest to Avra Valley. She learned about the unique features of various species of mesquite and how to market them. Sometimes she worked sixteen hours a day making, packaging, marketing, and selling tortillas. No matter who else tried to make mesquite tortillas—even with the same ingredients—Esperanza's were by far the best I had tasted.

I couldn't figure it out: Was the added flavor in the particular flour of the mesquite she had supplied to her and the way she kneaded it? Was it the way she really needed a job, and when mesquite offered her one, she expressed her gratitude through the mix of flours and oils she used and the way she used her hands? *Those hands.* They were hands that made little circular miracles out of a food as old as any in the desert.

One Sunday I was back in Tucson with a dozen Seri women who wanted to sell their baskets, their own hand-harvested and hand-ground mesquite meal and wild oregano at the farmers' market in Saint Phillip's Plaza. I had heard that Esperanza sometimes appeared there but often sold out of her product within an hour and drove home to be with her ailing father. When I looked for her among the vendors, she was nowhere to be seen.

I was breaking down the Seri display when someone came up and hugged me. It was Esperanza.

"Gary, it's working! I'm making a living off mesquite tortillas, up to 300 dozen a week. I'm now selling ten other products, too . . . things like almond mesquite cookies, spinach tortillas, and prickly pear cookies. They're in three to five different farmers' markets each week, several health food stores, and a diabetes clinic, with special orders from local customers and even shipping some to diabetics out of state. Six of us are working together, and we still can't keep up with the demand. I can't believe it!"

Esperanza hugged me again. And it felt like mesquite trees were hugging both of us.

MESQUITE

On my back and neck, I felt those hands. The ones that not only make magical tortillas but keep mesquite trees alive and in their place, reaching down into the depths of the earth hundreds of feet and bringing up flavors and fragrances to us that I'd never even imagined. Just who could have imagined such grace?

AFTERWORD

Beauty in Utility

No doubt my partner, Laurus nobilis, *has worried about my mental, emotional, and physical condition these last few months, as I have tried to decide whether to stay human or to continue on my transformation toward becoming a mesquite tree. She kindly made me an appointment with a doctor who practiced holistic medicine in Tucson. She felt that I needed examination thorough enough to determine just what had been causing these episodes of indecision and malaise during the previous few months.*

I was wary at first, when I found out he was not a tree doctor, but a physician who worked only on humans. But I went to the appointment anyway, sensing that I needed to honor the concerns of my lovely wife, who had stood by me throughout my dilemma.

At first the physician could find nothing unusual with my physical condition nor my motor responses. But then he noticed something in my hair that he found puzzling and decided to put me under with a sedative to be able to extract it.

When I awakened, he told me that he had trimmed back some of the hair on my crown, had taken some samples from my scalp, and had sent them off to a lab for analysis.

"We'll wait and see what the results say so that I may provide you with a definitive determination, but I think you may have a parasite. By the way, have you been out of the country lately or outdoors here where you might have been exposed to something unusual?"

"Well," I thought for a moment. "I haven't really been traveling much overseas lately, but I've had a couple trips to the deserts of Mexico, let's see . . . one of them to the Sonoran coast north of Kino . . . and one last spring or early summer to the Rio Grande, and another down at Organ Pipe Cactus, the national park just north of the border."

The doctor dutifully recorded this data on his notepad. "That's helpful. I think you may have a parasite, and when we get a determination of what it is, I just want to correlate its identity with what grows in the environments that you traveled to. I'll call you back within the next week."

Unsure of what would happen, I drove home and braced myself for the worst. Guinea worms? Zombie snails? Emerald jewel wasps? Sacculina barnacles? Giardia?

I sat down at my desk and pondered what kind of parasite might have taken over my body or my brain.

A cluster of mesquite pods hang down like fingers. I can see them from the window above my desk in the *casita* I use as my writing refuge on the edge of our orchard. They are the hands of time to me, warm and welcoming. They look almost as though they could be my own.

Come here, kid, they say, *let me scratch what itches you . . .*

I have begun to regard the particular mesquite tree on which those pods ripen to be an essential element of our orchard, of our lives. *It is family to me. It is my "blood."*

I realized that I could no longer think of mesquite as some noxious weed on the margins of my life or of our collective human existence. Whenever I feel down and out, I gravitate to its protective canopy, whether I sit below its trunk outside or view it from my mesquite-slab desk, where it frames my view of the world.

As a matter of fact, mesquite's presence in this place predates the pomegranates, figs, quinces, olives, and apples I intentionally planted to create our orchard and still out-produces all of those exotic trees.

That's right, it's my *pre-date* for the night. Its sinuous architectural form is far more pleasing than that of any other, albeit younger, trees.

And yet, I suppose, once a certain Mission olive sapling attains some stature, it might conceivably vie with the mesquite for the honor of being the loveliest tree in the entire orchard. It might reach such a status by the day I die. By the time that moment comes, however, they can roll my body downslope and bury me in the ground under a mesquite on the edge of the orchard, as ashes or compost for its future growth.

Mesquite has become a mainstay in my diet and in my aesthetics. I am afraid I cannot live without its loveliness, its attentiveness, or its usefulness.

With respect to the sheer loveliness of mesquite and a thousand other things, I have often pondered why mainstream America so often pits *utility* against *beauty*. Why would the economic value of a resource necessarily be diametrically opposed to the aesthetic value of the same being, plant, or animal?

It does not matter whether we consider beauty a purely visual phenomenon or one that involves all of our senses as well as our culture's symbolic meanings associated with them. Mesquite's architectural elegance, its fragrance, taste, and texture all spell beauty to me, writ large in the desert. It is not *merely* useful.

I am convinced that, at least as far as a mesquite tree goes, beauty and utility go hand in hand. Or limb with limb. They are my allies. We are not at war with one another.

Other cultures don't seem as fixated on such polarities. For the Maya, their sacred kapok tree is as impressive in the elegance of its towering architecture as it is in its many uses.

The same is true with the sacred blue, red, yellow, and white varieties of maize grown by the Navajo (or Diné). They are as lovely and useful in the daily fare found on the kitchen tables of the farming families that consume them as they are in the rain-bringing ceremonies of the spirits who help the Navajo live in balance—*nizhoni*—with their arid homelands.

And so I feel a certain remorse whenever I see a mesquite tree caught in the crossfire between those who wish to gain an income from its many products and those who wish to protect the tree for its grandeur, its intrinsic value, and its role in the ecological integrity of this arid landscape.

It seems our contemporary society is still struggling to see this tree in more than one light, as if we are incapable of acknowledging its chimerical qualities without succumbing to dualism.

That is why I find the mesquite tree to be a many-faceted persona in my life. It is kind of like a prism. Mesquite's arboreality is a radiant, translucent presence, whose meaning filters through many lenses, so that it refracts light in myriad ways.

Depending upon the emotional, economic, cultural, or spiritual perspective from which you look at it, a mesquite polarizes, reflects, or disperses the white light of its being in an altogether distinctive manner.

But if you always look at a mesquite from the same angle, you are likely to always see the same old tree through the same narrow bandwidth that taints most of your perceptions.

Instead, if we bend our minds to look at it from another angle, a broader rainbow of colors across the entire spectrum may be revealed to us.

As you may sense, I have recently had my own perceptions of mesquite reshuffled by several different factors. I've been infected by some mysterious parasite that the doctor hints is looming in my scalp and maybe in my brain. I suffered a serious concussion that disrupted my eye-to-brain neural transmitters. I am in residence on a piece of land where mesquite trees are seldom out of my view from dawn to dusk. And I still make frequent forays into mesquite-dominated landscapes with ranchers, quail hunters, wild foragers, woodcutters, and furniture makers.

I feel as if I have become a lump of stone placed in a tumbler, and all my old edges are wearing away.

Just after a desert dawn this last July, I witnessed a beautiful sight. As I walked down to the beach in a Seri Indian village, I caught out of the corner of my eye a slender young Seri Indian woman dressed in a blue shawl, yellow blouse, and long green skirt under the shadowy canopy of a mesquite tree. At first, I thought that she was raising her arms up high above her head as if in praise.

But then I realized that she was reaching for the ripened straw-colored pods of the mesquite, gathering up a bunch between her two hands, pulling them loose from the tree, then tossing them on a bright blue tarp, where she would dry them in the sun before grinding them into flour. A sea breeze made the branches above her head rock and bounce, and her arms and hands reached into the air in keeping with their rhythm. She stood barefoot, on her tippy-toes, swaying, as if waltzing with a taller partner.

Would this scene have been as beautiful if she had danced alone, without that tree as her partner? Or would it be as meaningful to me if she had merely been doing her dance, as play and not as work to feed her family? Or what if the tree had simply been swayed by the wind to drop its ripened pods to the ground without any human interacting with it? Why was that momentary collaboration so gorgeous in my mind's eye?

I think that the real beauty and the truly functional utility of this tree (and this world as a whole) lies in such collaborations, not in lives isolated from one another in a manner where we regard each living being as of value only as an entity unto itself.

The seventy-some kinds of native bees buzzing on the mesquite flowers outside my *casita* are one such collaboration: They make this semiarid landscape hum in multiple octaves just as resonant as the chants of Buddhist throat singers. The fiercely protective twig ants guarding the extrafloral nectaries of mesquites and acacias are another wondrous collaboration, as beautiful as they are functional.

Where does the value of their lives begin and where does the value of the life of a mesquite tree stop?

For all the assaults and insults that are hurled against them, the various mesquite species of North America—honey mesquite, velvet mesquite, and screwbean mesquite—have never really become endangered. They survive and thrive under conditions in which few others can stay alive.

I guess that it is time to admit that our society hasn't always dealt as lovingly and respectfully with mesquites as we ought to have. And yet, these trees are forgiving. They silently invite us back into their embraces, even when we have done them wrong.

At least for now, we are witnessing a surge in interest in what my old friend Petey Mesquitey calls the "growing native movement."

Many people of all shapes and colors are now making time and room for these trees, in order to dance with them in our desert landscapes once again.

The late Mark Moody of the Arizona Mesquite Company was one such nativist, a man who patiently spent years perfecting ways to cultivate jojoba bushes for their waxy nuts before turning to planting a mesquite plantation in Bouse, Arizona. He treated mesquite with as much or even more love and patience than he formerly showered upon his jojoba.

Up until his recent and untimely death, Mark grew row after row of mesquite trees for lumber, landscaping, and food. Muffin Burgess, the proprietor of Flor de Mayo Arts, offers her devoted clients at weekly farmers' markets in the Tucson vicinity a "delectable gluten-free mesquite flour grown sustainably in Arizona from our own native velvet mesquite" in Mark's memory.

Muffin makes her mesquite products from only the choicest and sweetest pods that are ground once, seed and all, cleaned, thoroughly dried, then ground again into a fine meal, uncooked. She has found mesquite meal to be excellent added to baked goods, smoothies, hot cereals, pancakes, and hot drinks. But the reach of her influence goes well beyond Arizona, for she is also in touch with Texan, New Mexican, and Sonoran mesquite food lovers, guiding them and training them in everything from food safety to the historic ethnobotanical uses of mesquites.

And yet Petey, Mark, and Muffin would have been the first to affirm that their interest in mesquite is not about its past grandeur in a now-degraded or partially restored landscape, but about the love they have for it and for the restorative roles it will play in the future of human health as well as in habitat health.

Along with *nopalitos* from the prickly pear cactus, mesquite flour now plays a major role in some indigenous and Hispanic communities in their fight to control the rising tide of adult-onset diabetes. Its galactomannan gums and soluble fiber dampens the blood sugar levels of diabetes-prone individuals and increases insulin sensitivity. It also reaches into the Anglo, Middle Eastern, African, and Asian immigrant communities, satisfying the "sweet tooth" in their young children without damaging their teeth, pancreas, and overall health the way that colas, chocolates, and high-fructose corn syrups do.

But we can't have mesquite available to restore our own health if we don't restore back to health a number of their many habitats. Mesquites need space, soil, and water to grow; for the last century, we have robbed them of all three ingredients.

And most of all, mesquite needs our unconditional love.

It is ironic that it has taken a major crisis in our own health status—propelled by the meteoric rise of obesity and diabetes among nearly all cultures now inhabiting the desert borderlands—for us to recognize that right on our very doorstep we have mesquites offering to be preventive medicines, salves, and cures for us. As nurse trees, they are willing to nurse *us* back to health.

But if mesquite is to become a significant part of our health care to protect us from the tsunami of diabetes rising in our midst, we must take better care of this humble, elegant tree.

I get all choked up just remembering and reciting the many wild rides that mesquite has taken with me, my wife, and many of our friends. They have been such steady allies . . . never abandoning me in my recent identity crisis. When I start to tear up thinking about them, I suddenly feel an urge to abandon my writing desk, to gather with friends to make an offering of thanksgiving on their behalf. And another one of thanksgiving, truth, and reconciliation for that impressive tree that has brought us all together into one community.

What else might we do to express our love for Mother Mesquite? Should we offer her water? Organic matter? Free rent until the end of time? Prayer? Confession? Expressions of redemption?

"Please forgive me, My Blossoming Lover, for all I have done and for all I have failed to do. May you go in peace, and may you grow as you please. Amen."

A telephone rings. It is my doctor.

"I'm afraid I have what I think is some bad news for you. You have some kind of parasite that we've never detected before at our hospital.

We found both some sticky seeds attached to your hair follicles and some green parasitic growths that began at the skin of your scalp and now appear to be invading your brain. When we did some tests to determine their identity, the results came back that they are of a hemiparasite know to science as Phorodendron californicum."

I screamed with delight, not horror.

"Yes, I know that species. It is a growth that desert naturalists call 'desert mistletoe.' You know, mesquite *mistletoe. I've made it! I'VE MADE IT!"*

The doctor seemed confused. I was not sure that he was still on the phone. Then he asked, "Made what?"

"I've made it across the threshold! I've reached paradise!"

ACKNOWLEDGMENTS

Thanks to so many friends and so many trees. First and foremost to Laura Smith Monti, who has spent more time with me pondering mesquite and love than anyone else in my life. Any resemblance to the character *Laurus nobilis* in these pages is completely coincidental. To Barbara Ras, who started me on this journey, but didn't fully get where it had to go. Blessings, Barbara, anyway. To Paul Martin, Richard Felger, Carolyn Niethammer, Julian Hayden, Carlos Martinez del Rio, Amadeo Rea, and Ray Turner, thank you for initiating me into the deep history of mesquite more than a quarter century ago. To Petey Mesquitey, aka Peter Gierlach, thank you for the foreword and for reminding me that botany and humor go together well, as I've always known in my heart. To Clifford Pablo, Hugh Fitzsimons, Juan Olmedo, Jordan Golubov, Art and Valerie Flores, Ed Fredrickson, Dennis Moroney, Martha Burgess, Ivan Aguirre, Esperanza Arevalo, Brad Lancaster, Tony Burgess, Barbara Rose, Jeau Allen, Bill Doelle, Connie Barlow, Wendy Hodgson, Kay Fowler, Paul Mirocha, Gabriel Escalante, Dave Perino, Sunny Savage, Vince Kana'i Dodge, Stephen Paul, Steve Archer, Steve Buchmann, Barry Infuso, Chuck Weber, Vaughn Bryant, Austin Long, Julio Betancourt, Tom Van Devender, Jennie Brand-Miller, Peter Felker, Humberto Suzan, Josh Tewksbury, Carlos Martinez del Rio, Justin Schmidt, Cristina Monroy, and the entire Comcáac community, thank you for being such generous mentors with regard to mesquite. I am grateful to Serena Milano at Slow Food International, as well as to Laurie Monti, Mike Gray, and Gay Chanler for helping us board fire-roasted mesquite flour from the Seri Indian (Comcáac) community onto the International Ark of Taste. And to the loving memory of Paul Martin and Mark Moody, Juanita Ahill and Frances Manual, Delores Lewis and Ruth Giff, Jim Berry and Julian Hayden, Laura Kerman and Jose Kerman, Amalia Astorga and Becky Moser, pioneering Mesquiteers of the first class.

No mesquite trees were harmed in the making of this book.

RECIPES

Mesquite Molasses
Melaza de la Péchita del Mezquite
Dibs bi al-Kharoub Amriki

Yield: 2½ to 3 pints

Once you recognize that mesquite pods are essentially the New World analog of the pods of carob (also known as locust or St. John's bread), you can begin to adapt dozens of delicious Middle Eastern and North African recipes to mesquite pods. Most of these call for use of pod fragments in infusions or for toasted pods ground into a fine powderlike flour. The Arabic term for carob pods of the tree *Ceratonia siliqua* is *al-kharoub.* It gave rise to the ancient Latin *carrubium,* which was Hispanicized as *algarroba* and Anglicized as **carob.** Mesquites (not just carob trees) are still called algarroba in most of South America and in regions of Mexico as well.

For the infused broth (makes 4 or 5 cups):
18 cups of water
6 cups dried mesquite pods (about 48 ounces),
    cracked into 2-inch fragments
1 teaspoon coarsely ground sea salt or kosher salt

For the molasses:
3 cups clarified, infused mesquite broth (from above)
⅓ of a 1.7–2.0 ounce packet of powdered pectin
    (or 1 cup powdered *tejocote,* dried Mexican hawthorn fruit)
4 cups raw turbinado sugar (or 4 tablespoons dried,
    powdered stevia leaves)
4 tablespoons sour orange or lime juice
Olive oil, as needed

1. Begin by making a simple infusion of the dried, cracked mesquite pods in water. Place the water in a large nonreactive pot, add the mesquite pod pieces, and bring to a boil. Reduce the heat, and simmer the mixture for an hour, skimming off any froth and fibrous pieces of the pods. Add the salt and stir to dissolve.
2. Strain through a long-handled colander, wire-mesh strainer, or a cheesecloth bag, catching and disposing of the remaining pod fiber and mushy meal, while retaining the somewhat translucent, slightly opaque infused broth. Pour into a 1-gallon glass jar, cap, and cool in a refrigerator or on ice in a sink for an hour. Gently pour into jars through a finer mesh strainer, catching any remaining sediment or dregs of the solids in the screen and keeping the flavorful amber liquid.
3. To make the molasses, place 3 cups of this clarified, infused broth in a nonreactive saucepan with the powdered pectin or hawthorn powder. Slowly bring to a boil, stirring constantly with a wooden spoon, while adding turbinado sugar (or stevia powder) and the citrus juice of your choice. After the mixture has boiled for 2 minutes, pour into hot, sterilized glass jars, top with ⅛ inch of olive oil, and seal the lids. Place the jars on a towel and let cool in a refrigerator, where the slightly tangy syrup will thicken.
4. Use as a glaze, as a syrup over shaved ice, in spritzers of one-fifth molasses and four-fifths fizzy water, or in the Mesquite Molasses–Tahini Dipping Sauce (see page 180) to serve with pita bread, crackers, or bagel chips.

Mesquite Molasses–Tahini Dipping Sauce
Melaza del Mezquite con Ajonjoli
Dibs bi Mezquite, Tahini

Yield: 1 cup

Dipping sauces for raw vegetables and chips are increasingly popular today, but have ancient origins. They are often prepared from a highly storable thick paste like harissa or tahini, to which lemon juice, oil, yogurt, or water are added. This one capitalizes on both sweet and savory dimensions of mesquite.

½ cup mesquite molasses
½ cup sesame tahini paste
4 tablespoons lemon juice
Olive oil, as needed

1. In a wide-mouthed ceramic bowl, mix the mesquite molasses and tahini and begin to beat with a wooden spoon, slowly adding the lemon juice. As the ingredients begin to fuse, whip with a twisting motion of your wrist until the sauce begins to froth.
2. Serve in the same bowl as a tangy dipping sauce with plain pita bread, with warm pita drizzled or brushed with olive oil and sprinkled with zaatar spice mixture, or with crackers or bagel chips. To store overnight, top with a sheen of olive oil.

Mesquite Shrub Syrup
Jarabe de la Péchita del Mezquite
Sharab al-Kharroub Amriki

Yield: 9 to 12 cups

The Spanish term for lighter syrups, **jarabe,** is derived from the Arabic term **al-Kharroub** for carob and its syrups, as are the English terms **syrup, sorbet, sherbet,** and **shrub.**

1 pound (about ½ gallon in volume) of dried, toasted mesquite
    pods (rendering about 3 cups of juicy mash)
8 cups distilled water
3 cups raw turbinado sugar

1. Place the mesquite pods in a large nonreactive soup pot or slow cooker and add the distilled water. Simmer for 45 minutes until the pods are soft and somewhat mushy.
2. Remove them from the pot with a slotted spoon, then squeeze them through the mesh of a grade 50 heavy cotton cheesecloth bag or through a colander into a nonreactive saucepan. You should have about 3 to 4 cups of mesquite puree to use.
3. Add the turbinado sugar to the mesquite puree and bring this liquid in the saucepan back to a steady simmer, stirring gently to avoid sticking. Let it bubble while stirring for 10 to 15 minutes, until the mesquite puree and sugar are fully integrated into a light, smooth syrup. Add more distilled water if needed to thin.
4. Strain through a colander and cool. Use a funnel to pour the shrub syrup into sterilized glass jars seven-eighths of the way to the mouths, seal the lids immediately, and store in the fridge. Add more water to maintain the liquid as a light syrup as needed. Serve cold.

Kiawe Kooler
Mesquite Shrub Spritzer
Licuado del Mezquite

One beverage you can make from your mesquite shrub is what my mesquite-loving friends in Hawai'i—Sunny Savage and Vince Kana'i Dodge—call Kiawe Cooler. **Kiawe** is the native Hawaiian name for the dominant mesquite, *Prosopis pallida*, that was introduced to the dry sides of several islands. **Kiawe** has been translated as "a pillar" or "a being that is swaying." Here is my adaptation of Sunny's recipe from her delightful book, *Wild Food Plants of Hawai'i*.

9 cups mesquite shrub syrup, or 4 cups mesquite pods,
    broken into 2-inch fragments
2 tablespoons lemon or orange outer rind (zest)
10 cups distilled water
6 wild cinnamon leaves
6 wild allspice leaves
Mesquite honey, to taste
4 cups fizzy soda water
Lemon or lime peel twist
Shaved ice

1. If you do not have mesquite shrub syrup on hand, then soak mesquite pod fragments and citrus rind in a saucepan of water overnight. In the morning, add the spice leaves and mesquite honey, then simmer the mixture, making sure that it does not reach the boiling point. After an hour and a half on low heat, strain through a colander into jars or bottles, then cap. Refrigerate.

2. To make one kooler: Add one part chilled syrup to four parts fizzy water, with a lemon or lime peel twist on the rim of the glass.

RECIPES

Mesquite Atole
Atole de la Péchita del Mezquite
Mezquitatol

Yield: about 2 quarts

Atole is one of the oldest and richest beverages of Mesoamerica, whether fermented or not. This version allows for brief fermentation with powdered yeast culture. Or, if you are lucky, you can culture the naturally occurring yeasts that have already colonized clay *olla* pots made by certain tribes in the US Southwest and Mexico for brewing *tesguino* corn or agave beers or *tepache* and *colonche* fruit punches. *Mezquitatol* is the Hispanicized conjugation of two Nahuatl words used for mesquite trees and their pods and for the resulting beverage. Mesquite is still used in atoles and pinoles in many places in the Chihuahuan Desert, particularly around the "la Laguna" region of Torreón, Coahuila.

1 gallon dried and toasted mesquite pods
Water to cover 1 tablespoon ground allspice or 2 allspice berries
2 tablespoons ground cinnamon or 1 cinnamon stick
1 tablespoon vanilla extract or vanilla puree
Pinch of salt
Pinch of brewer's yeast

1. In a large slow cooker or open *olla,* soak the pods in water overnight, then warm them over low heat the next morning for an hour. Pour the softened pods into a grade 50 heavy cotton cheesecloth bag placed over a sink, draining away most of the liquid.
2. Mash the pods through the cheesecloth back into the slow cooker or *olla,* adding the allspice, cinnamon, vanilla, salt, and brewer's yeast. Let sit for another day in the sun, with more cheesecloth tightly stretched over the mouth of the pot and secured with a rubber band.
3. The atole can be served hot or cold in mugs, with cinnamon or sweet chile powder sprinkled on top.

Mesquite and Fermented Fruit Shrub Beverage
Tepache del Mezquite
Mezquitepache

Yield: 4 to 6 servings

Tepache, an ancient Mesoamerican tradition of mildly fermented beverages, is now reappearing in bars and cantinas throughout the US and Mexico. For good reason: drinking these pleasant, highly nutritious probiotic drinks simply makes you feel better! They're not all that different from the sharab or shrub drinks previously mentioned, but typically include fresh fruits such as pineapples or the fruit of barrel cactus (*bisnagas*).

1 pineapple or 6 to 8 ripe yellow barrel-cactus fruits
Distilled water to cover
½ cup raw turbinado sugar or shaved *panela* from a *piloncillo* cone
1 cup lukewarm water
½ cup mesquite shrub syrup (see page 181)
1 cinnamon stick
3 or 4 whole cloves

1. Skin the pineapple or the barrel-cactus fruits and place the peels in a half-gallon mason jar or glass pitcher. Add distilled water to cover the fruit peels.
2. Dissolve the turbinado sugar or the shaved panela in the lukewarm water, stir, then pour into the jar or pitcher. Add the mesquite shrub syrup, cinnamon, and cloves, then stir.
3. Cover with a cheesecloth tightly stretched over the mouth of the jar or pitcher and secure with a rubber band. Let sit at room temperature for 3 to 5 days, sampling it with a ladle after the third day.
4. When the flavor shifts from sweet to tartly tangy, it is ready to drink. Pour the *tepache* through a fine mesh metal strainer through a funnel into sterilized jars or bottles with tight lids. Refrigerate, or serve cool in iced mugs.

Fermented Prickly Pear Cactus Punch with Mesquite Flavoring
Colonche con la Péchita del Mezquite Navaita

Yield: 8 to 10 servings

Colonche is a sweet, naturally fizzy pre-Hispanic fermented beverage based on the use of *tuna,* the red, purple, or orange fruit of prickly pear cacti (*Opuntia* spp.). Cultivated fruit of *tuna* and the kefir grains on their skin are favored for this beverage, but the fruit of other prickly pear species and even the *pitahaya* of columnar cacti (*Carnegiea, Stenocereus,* and *Pachycereus*) can be used as flavorings. In this recipe, we used toasted mesquite pod flour as a sweetener, along with the cactus fruit itself. In preparing *colonche,* fully ripened cactus fruits are peeled and their pulp crushed to obtain a sticky, slightly mucilaginous juice, which is then boiled and condensed for 2 to 3 hours. After cooling, the juice is inoculated with either a cup of an older batch of *colonche* or with a special fermentation starter called *tibicos. Tibicos* form gelatinous masses of yeasts and bacteria that remind me of sourdough starters or vinegar mothers and are cultured in small clay containers of water with brown sugar (*panela or panocha from piloncillos*). The yeast in *tibicos* is not just one more unique indigenous Mexican strain of brewer's yeast (as in *teguino* and *tepache*), but an entirely different species named *Torulopsis taboadae.* Depending on temperatures, fermentation usually takes just 2 to 4 days; longer times in the fermentation pot or bowl often move the beverage toward a tangier vinegar flavor.

4 ½ pounds mature *tuna* (prickly pear cactus fruit)
    or other cactus fruit
1 cup warm distilled water
⅔ teaspoon of active dry yeast powder (or use *tibicos* or older
    colonche as starter)
¼ cup mesquite molasses or shrub syrup
Shaved ice, as needed

Splash of lime juice per glass

1. Peel the cactus fruit to obtain their juicy fruit pulp in one of three ways:

   - Using a paring knife, hold the fruit upright with a fork or one finger (placed between the spines) and trim the skin in a spiral by spinning the fruit;
   - Cut off the ends, slit the skin from top to bottom, and remove it; or
   - Place the whole fruit in a blender and run it on high for 30 seconds.

2. Pour the juice and pulp through a fine mesh strainer or a grade 50 heavy cotton cheesecloth bag placed atop a bowl and squeeze the juice out of it, leaving the seeds, spines, prickly glochids, and pulp behind. Crush any remaining pulp solids squeezed out of the strainer or bag with a mortar and pestle and pour the macerated pulp and all the juice into a glass bowl or clay *olla* pot.

3. In a smaller bowl, mix the warm water with the yeast or *tibico* starter, then stir in the mesquite molasses or shrub syrup. Pour this starter into the larger glass bowl or clay pot with the cactus juice, then cover with cheesecloth or a cotton towel. Secure the cover with a rubber band or string. Let sit at room temperature in a shady place in a kitchen or root cellar for 2 to 4 days, waiting for bubbling to decline. Sample each day after the second day to ensure that bacterial fermentation is not making it too tangy, sour, or vinegarlike. Pour into jars or bottles, cap, and refrigerate until ready to drink.

4. Serve with shaved ice and a splash of lime juice.

Mesquite Tamales
Tamal de la Péchita del Mezquite
Mezquitamal

Yield: 1 dozen large or 2 dozen small tamales (about 6 servings)

My friends Chef Molly Beverly and Carolyn Niethammer have helped revive and modernize one of the most ancient Mesoamerican uses of mesquite—its inclusion with cornmeal in tamale batter, or *masa,* that is then wrapped in corn husks, banana leaves, or yerba santa leaves. Here, I've adapted Molly's recipe to include a few more desert surprises embedded in the masa itself, as many sweet holiday tamales feature during the Christmas and Hanukkah season.

To gain the full flavor, texture, and nutritive value of tamales, it is best to find someone in your own community who uses the traditional *nixtamal* processing of corn with culinary ash or *cal* (lime) or learn it on your own, rather than succumbing to industrially processed *maseca,* a poor substitute. The sweetness that the mesquite flour imparts to tamales provides a perfect match for a warm and savory green sauce of tomatillos, diced long green chile peppers, or a *mole verde.*

For the tamales:
12 large cornhusks or 24 small ones
Water to cover

For the masa:
2 cups fire-toasted mesquite pod flour
2 cups fresh nixtamalized corn masa
1 tablespoon White Sonora wheat 00 pastry flour (optional)
1 teaspoon baking powder or culinary (saltbush) ash
¼ teaspoon salt
½ cup unsalted, softened butter
1 cup water
1 teaspoon Fremont's wolfberries or sun-dried goji berries
1 teaspoon desert hackberries

1 teaspoon bits of cracked nonbitter *bellota* acorns
1 teaspoon finely chopped wild green chiltepín peppers
1 teaspoon Arizona or New Mexico cracked pistachio kernels

1. Loosen stacked cornhusks from one another, place in a large bowl, and cover with water. Assemble a pot to serve as a steamer, with 3 inches of water at the bottom, and with a colander or strainer nested into it above the water level. Heat the water to a simmer.
2. In a second glass bowl, mix mesquite flour, corn masa, wheat flour (optional), baking powder, and salt. Add butter and water, then mix into a thick batter. Spread a quarter inch of freshly nixtamalized masa, then add baking powder or culinary ash. Beat in softened butter and water to make a dough that is thoroughly moist (like pudding) but not runny. Add the berries, cracked nut kernels, and green chiltepín peppers to the dough, dispersing them throughout the mix.
4. Next, remove the rehydrated cornhusks and pat dry with a towel. Lay them all out on a counter with their narrowest ends pointing away from you. With a spatula, spread ¼ inch of dough filling across each cornhusk, leaving the top third near the narrow end uncovered. Fold the right, then the left sides of the husk over the filling in toward the middle. Now, close the tamale by folding down the top pointed end with one sharp crease. Place the fully assembled tamale folded-side down on a baking sheet and align the others next to the first. Take each tamale from the pan and stand them on their ends in the steamer, folded side down and open side up. Cover the pot tightly so no steam will escape. Steam the tamales over the simmering water for 45 minutes, then remove them from the heat and let sit for 3 to 5 minutes before serving.
5. Garnish with your choice of warmed, freshly made tomatillo sauce, chunky green chile pepper sauce, *mole verde,* or grated *queso fresco.*

Mesquite-Crusted Quail with Chipotle Cream Gravy

Cordoniz Empanizada con Panko y Péchita en Crema del Chipotle Jalapeño

Yield: 6 servings

Chicken-fried steak or quail was never much of attraction for me, until I began to sample the terrific renditions emerging out of the Big Bend region. Across West Texas, chefs are featuring pecan-, pistachio-, or mesquite-crusted steaks, poultry, or game birds that are bathed in a jalapeño or chipotle cream gravy. The mesquite flour and panko crust together offer a crunchy texture and smoky flavor that is hard to beat. A simple jalapeño cream gravy can be substituted for this chipotle cream sweetened with prickly pear or pomegranate syrup. With either gravy, drizzling it on the bird rather than drowning it better maintains the crunch and punch of the quail itself.

For the quail:
½ cup White Sonora wheat flour
1 cup mesquite pod flour
2 cups panko (Japanese-style) bread crumbs
1 tablespoon kosher salt
1 tablespoon freshly ground black pepper
1 tablespoon Chile Caribe flakes or cayenne pepper
2 eggs, beaten
½ cup buttermilk or cream
6 semi-boneless quail, pounded and butterflied
Canola oil

For the chipotle cream gravy (makes 1 cup):
¼ cup red wine
2 tablespoons prickly pear or pomegranate syrup
¼ cup mesquite shrub syrup (see page 181)
1 large chipotle pepper in adobo sauce, finely chopped

1 teaspoon sea salt or coarse kosher salt
¼ teaspoon freshly ground black pepper
1 cup heavy cream

1. Preheat the oven to 350 degrees F.
2. In a one small bowl, mix the flours, panko, salt, pepper, and chile flakes. In another, beat the eggs and buttermilk to make a wash. Then dip each butterflied quail in the wash, thoroughly moistening the skin. Next dredge it through the panko and flours, coating it with a crust.
3. Put about an inch of canola oil in the bottom of a heavy-bottomed skillet and warm on medium heat. When the oil is simmering, place the quail in the pan. You may need to do more than one batch. Shake the pan gently to keep the crusted quail from sticking and fry for 3 minutes on each side until golden brown on both sides. Add more oil to the pan between fryings, if necessary.
4. Place the quail on a baking pan and bake in the oven for 5 to 7 minutes to finish cooking.
5. To make the gravy, heat the red wine and prickly pear or pomegranate syrup in a deep-sided, heavy-bottomed 12-inch skillet over medium heat. When the wine sauce begins to bubble, add the chipotle pepper, salt, and black pepper, and stir for about 2 minutes until smooth. Lower the heat, then whisk in the heavy cream.
6. Remove from heat, strain through a fine metal mesh strainer into a serving bowl. Place each quail on a separate plate, drizzle the chipotle cream gravy over each, and serve while warm. Serve with Sweet and Spicy Maguey and Mesquite Molasses-Glazed Coleslaw (see page 191) as a side dish.

Sweet and Spicy Maguey and Mesquite Molasses–Glazed Coleslaw
Ensalada Mixta con Salsa de Melazas de Mezquite y Maguey

Yield: 8 servings as a side dish

This coleslaw is a great complement to barbecued meats, spicy foods, and cold drinks! It draws upon both mesquite and maguey molasses to glaze a colorful mix of raw vegetables, fruits, and nuts in a sweet and spicy vinaigrette.

For the vinaigrette:
1 cup chipotle chiles in adobo sauce
¼ cup apple cider vinegar
2 tablespoons maguey sweet sap molasses (or, if unavailable, dark agave nectar)
2 tablespoons Mesquite Molasses (see page 178)
2 tablespoons freshly squeezed lime juice
⅓ cup water
1½ teaspoons sea salt

For the coleslaw:
2 ounces peeled and shredded jicama, soaked in lime juice
1 chayote squash or crisp Beit Alpha cucumber (about 5 ounces)
⅓ cup pineapple chunks
⅓ cup pecan nut pieces (or slivered almonds)
½ cup Napa cabbage leaves
Sea salt
½ cup fresh pomegranate arils (kernels)

1. For the vinaigrette, combine the chiles, vinegar, both kinds of molasses, lime juice, water, and salt in a blender and process at high speed until a thick liquid glaze forms. Add more water to the blender if the mixture is too sticky to easily spoon into a glass bowl. Set aside.

2. Meanwhile, soak the shredded jicama root in lime juice to cover in a small bowl.

3. In a saucepan, cover the chayote squash with water and boil until it is tender but still firm, drain, and place on a cutting board. Slice in half from top to bottom, then incise and spoon out the two halves of its large seed. Let cool, then peel and shred or grate into the bowl with the jicama. Add the pineapple chunks and stir together.

4. In a lightly oiled frying pan, toast the nuts until they are lightly browned, about 4 minutes over medium heat. Set aside to cool.

5. On the cutting board, cut the Napa cabbage in half, incise the tougher core, and slice into long ruffled strips.

6. Just before serving, combine the cabbage strips with the chayote and jicama shreds with pineapple chunks and toasted nuts in a large salad bowl, and toss with the vinaigrette, adding salt to taste. Serve heaped conically on small plates and garnish with pomegranate arils on top for color.

Mesquite Mole Enchiladas with Wild Greens and Nuts

Enchiladas de Mole y Mezquite con Quelites y Nueces

Yield: 4 servings

Enchiladas and *entomatadas* have probably been evolving for centuries, ever since the first plump little corn tortillas were smeared with *molli* spice mixtures that had been ground into pastes in stone mortars called *molcajetes.* Mesquite pod flour happens to be a perfect ingredient for enhancing *mole* sauces, given its satisfying blend of savory and sweet flavors and fragrances. My friend Amy Valdés Schwemm has been experimenting with mixing mesquite into *mole dulce* sauces for years, applying it to turkey, chicken, squash, mushroom, and cheese fillings in enchiladas. Amy's microenterprise, *Mano y Metate*, offers her *mole dulce* both online and at farmers' markets in southern Arizona, but its blend of chocolates, chiles, almonds, dried fruits, and spices is representative of other *moles* and *recaudos* that many of you can find in Mexico or the United States (or make yourself). For this purpose, we will let you select your *mole* of choice, and I will focus on the other ingredients for these delicious enchiladas that I have adapted from Amy's groundwork.

3 tablespoons canola oil, divided, plus more for frying
1 cup sweet *mole* paste or powder of your choice
2 tablespoons toasted mesquite pod flour
1½ cups chicken broth or vegetable broth
Salt to taste
2 teaspoons cracked pistachio kernels
2 teaspoons cracked pecan nuts
2 teaspoons almond slices
1 cup wild amaranth leaves (*quelites de las aguas* or *huazontles*)
1 cup diced Texas sweet onion
1 cup *queso fresco* or any fresh farmer's cheese, crumbled
12 thick corn tortillas

1. Preheat the oven to 375 degrees F.
2. In a nonstick saucepan, heat 2 tablespoons of the canola oil, slowly adding the *mole* powder or paste and mesquite flour and stirring frequently to avoid scorching, sticking, or smoking. As the oil, powder, and flour blend into a thick, dark paste, slowly add the broth. Continue to stir as the sauce thickens and simmers, adding more broth any time it gets too thick and sticky. Add salt to taste, then set aside to cool.
3. Next, add a bit of the remaining oil to another skillet and toast the pistachios, pecans, and almonds until golden brown. While they are toasting, finely chop the wild amaranth greens and dice the sweet onion on a cutting board. Add the rest of the oil and the greens and onion to the skillet. As they begin to fry, mix in the crumbled soft cheese until it melts and set this mixture aside.
4. In another, smaller skillet, pour ½ inch of canola oil, bring to medium heat, and drop a corn tortilla in, keeping it in the oil for just a few seconds on each side. Just as it becomes soft and pliable from the oil, lift it out with tongs or a pancake turner and dry on a plate covered with paper towels. Each tortilla is swiftly fried in this manner until it is pliable; stack it on top of the others on the plate.
5. Next, place a casserole dish in the open oven that is now at 375 degrees F. Use tongs to dredge each tortilla through the *mole* and mesquite sauce in the saucepan, coating both sides. Place in an oiled casserole dish one at a time. With a wooden spoon, place 2 tablespoons of the greens, onion, nuts, and cheese mixture in a narrow band across each tortilla, roll slightly, creasing a seam in its midsection, and place the seam-side down, edging it up against the side of the casserole dish. Continue filling the casserole dish with filled and folded tortillas stacked side by side, then pour the *mole* and mesquite sauce over all of them. They are now enchiladas!
6. Cover the dish with a lid and place in the oven for 20 minutes. Remove the lid for the last 2 minutes to allow a crispier texture to emerge. Remove from the oven, cool for 3 or 4 minutes, and serve.

HARVESTING
AND PROCESSING
OF MESQUITE PODS
FOR FOOD

Harvesting and processing mesquite pods (we are not after the seeds inside them!) is far less problematic than doing the same for pecans, walnuts, pawpaws, or persimmons, but newcomers to the desert often seem daunted by the task. Do not fear: Help is on the way. There is no need to get harvester's cramps over joining the profession of *Prosopis* pod pickers and pounders. Mesquite milling is far easier than positioning yourself for your first kiss.

Selecting Your Harvesting Site

Site selection and preparation are everything. First, avoid harvesting pods adjacent to fields, roadsides, or rangelands that are sprayed with herbicides. Dry washes or ephemeral watercourses not far from parking areas are ideal sites to seek out, since they usually have more productive trees than upland vegetation. As you see pods begin to ripen from green to a tawny or rosy hue in the spring or summer, begin to choose the gathering grounds where you wish to forage. First, remember where you or others have sampled the sweetest and most flavorful pods in previous years, for all mesquite trees are not equal in taste. Next, look for larger trees with higher densities of pods, so you don't spend all of your foraging time walking around looking for the mother lode. When you've selected a site, prune back any broken or dead lower branches of the tree that may get in the way of your reach once you begin the harvest.

Timing Your Harvest

To avoid moldy pods, the best time to harvest pods is before the summer monsoons, which typically begin between June 20 and July 10. Frequently check on the pace of pod ripening over the season in order to schedule your harvesting foray when more than half the pods on most trees are so ripe that you can simply brush them and they "dehisce," or fall from the branches. They often begin to become mottled with red and exude a sugary syrup onto their surfaces. *Tasting a fresh pod or two from each tree before you harvest a lot of pods* is the best way to ensure that you devote your time to the most flavorful ones available on the site.

As I am checking the trees in the weeks leading up to this stage, I often put inexpensive tarps out on the ground under the canopies of the best trees or, better yet, hang some bird netting made to protect fruit trees from feathered foes from the lowest branches. In other words, *do everything possible to avoid picking any pods up directly off the ground* to maintain the highest food safety standards. And to the extent that it is possible, choose to harvest pods before heavy rains, not after them, as that is when the pods tend to spoil, discolor, and attract fungal spores that lead to aflatoxins or other health risks.

On the day of harvesting, bring along some lightweight baskets or plastic paint cans, carefully washed and dried before use. Wear long-sleeved shirts, gloves, and sturdy shoes that will repel any thorns in the understory. Some harvesters use small handheld garden rakes or other implements to brush the pods into buckets or baskets, but I simply brush them into my baskets with my fingers. Immediately after each brushing, remove leaf rachises, twigs, and other debris from your container before adding more pods to it. You may have to do cleaning and sorting a second time once you bring the pods out of the field, but begin to reduce nonpod litter while you are under the trees.

The Desert Harvesters project that one person can leisurely pick 5 gallons of whole pods from a pruned-up mesquite tree (without picking any pods up off the ground) in about eighty minutes. It takes another fifteen minutes to lay out the pods to dry, clean them, and store them for milling. The 5 gallons of whole pods can be ground into about 250 to 300 ounces of flour, or 3.25 to 3.75 pounds of edible product.

Drying, Toasting, and Milling

Keep in mind that it will take another half hour or so to dry (preferably toast) and mill each 5-gallon batch of whole pods. Once you are back where you wish to store and potentially mill the pods, dump the basket loads and bucket loads out on a clean tarp, and sort out any green, withered, animal-damaged, or discolored pods. *That same day*, begin drying the pods out. For small batches, you can obviously oven dry them spread out on baking pans in low heat. Other harvesters construct a 4-foot by 8-foot solar dryer, placing stainless steel hardware cloth or other mesh at the bottom of a 2-by-4-foot frame covered with glazing. The Seri Indian women we work with toast the pods over a 2-foot-wide by 6-foot-long bed of mesquite charcoal, using a rake to move the fully toasted and dried ones off to the side. Using this traditional process as a point of departure, we have purchased small-scale chile pepper roasters, which are barrel-like tumblers covered with a tight steel mesh where the pods are passed in front of a propane-fueled torch. This not only dries the pods down quickly, but also toasts them so that, when milled, the particle size of the flour is finer and the flavor more aromatic, like mesquite smoke. It also kills nearly all bruchid beetles that lay eggs in pods otherwise left undried in storage. I prefer the tabletop chile roasters in the Arizona Chile Roasters line fabricated by McBroom Metal Works in Tucson.

As far as milling goes, hammer mills are the best choice for milling mesquite flour, and the Meadows Mills No. Five model has become the mill of choice for milling managed by community co-ops or nonprofits. An operating manual for these larger-scale mesquite pod mills ($4,000 to $6,000 per mill) can be found on the Desert Harvester's website, www.desertharvesters.org/hammermill. However, South American *algarroba* millers of mesquite flour use less expensive ($700 to $800) tabletop hammer mills that can easily process several kilos or pounds per hour. If hammer mills of any kind are out of your price range, other flour mills will work if the pods are broken into pieces and toasted so that they are extremely brittle and easy to pulverize. They nevertheless gum up the mills enough to require frequent cleaning. Heavy-duty blenders work, but they are vulnerable to gumming up and tine damage. Then, of course, you can always go the low-tech route with a *mano* grindstone and a *metate* pestle.

Whichever kind of mill you use, sifting out seeds and partially broken chunks of pods from the flour is necessary. This process seldom takes more than two siftings. The resulting sifted flour must be stored under dry conditions where humidity does not change much over the season, or else the moist flour will gum up into hard cake-like chunks. Triple-ply bags or double layers of airtight, food-grade hard plastic storage containers with desiccant between the two walls work best.

For more terrific information about the volumes, weights, and processes for milling pods, see the Desert Harvesters' 2016 book *Eat Mesquite and More* or visit their website, beginning on this page: www.desertharvesters.org/how-we-run-mesquite-millings/time-volume-value-of-pod-harvests.

For those of you who wish to use the pods for beverages rather than mill them into flour, you can simply infuse dried, broken pod fragments in water, preferably by placing them in a cheesecloth bag, soaking, and then pressing their moist mash through the cloth and discarding the larger contents remaining in the bag.

FURTHER READING

Ansley, R. J., T. W. Boutton, and P. W. Jacoby. "Root Biomass and Distribution Pattern in a Semiarid Mesquite Savanna: Responses to Long-Term Rainfall Manipulation." *Rangelands Ecology Management* 67 (2014): 2096–215.

Austin, Daniel. *Baboquivari Mountain Plants: Identification, Ecology, and Ethnobotany.* Tucson: University of Arizona Press, 2010.

Barlow, Connie. *The Ghosts of Evolution: Nonsensical Fruit, Missing Partners and Other Ecological Anachronisms.* New York: Basic Books/ Perseus Group, 2000.

Brown, Joel B., and Steve Archer. "Shrub Invasion of Grassland: Recruitment Is Continuous and Not Regulated by Herbaceous Biomass or Density." *Ecology* 80, no. 7 (1999): 2385–96.

Campbell, Steve. "TCU's Prairie Prophet Taught 'Urban Shamans' about Life and Mortality." *Fort Worth Star-Telegram,* May 20, 2013. www .star-telegram.com/2013/05/20/4869738/tcus-prairie-prophet -taught-urban.html

Capra, Fritzjof, and Pier Luigi Luisi. *The Systems of Life: A Unifying Vision.* Cambridge, UK: Cambridge, University Press, 2014.

Cassady, Frederic G., and Joan Houston Hall. *Dictionary of American Regional English,* vol. 3, *I–O.* Cambridge, MA: Belknap Press of Harvard University, 1996.

Chamowitz, Daniel. *What a Plant Knows: A Field Guide to the Senses.* New York: Scientific American/Farrar, Straus and Giroux, 2012.

Cheatham, Scooter, and Marshall C. Johnston, with Lynn Marshall. *Useful Plants of Texas.* Austin: Useful Plants, Inc., 2000.

Davis, Owen. "Climate and Vegetation Patterns in Surface Samples from Arid Western U.S.A.: Application to Holocene Climatic Reconstructions." *Palynology* 19 (1995): 97–120.

Del Barco, Miguel. *The Natural History of Baja California.* Frank Tiscareno, ed. Los Angeles: Dawson's Book Shop, 1980.

Desert Harvesters. *Eat Mesquite and More: A Cookbook.* Foreword by Gary Paul Nabhan. Tucson, AZ: Desert Harvesters/Green Book Initiative, 2017.

Felger, Richard S. "Mesquite in Indian Cultures of Southwestern North America." In Beryl B. Simpson, *Mesquite: Its Biology in Two Desert Scrub Ecosystems.* Stroudsburg, PA: Dowden, Hutchinson and Ross, 1977.

Felker, Peter. "Mesquite Flour: New Life for an Ancient Staple." *Gastronomica* 5, no. 2 (2005): 85–89.

Flannery, Tim. Introduction in Peter Wohlleben, *The Hidden Life of Trees.* Vancouver, BC: Greystone Press with David Suzuki Institute, 2015.

Fowler, Kay. "Plant 'Wifery' in the Great Basin: Indigenous and Diffused," presented at *XVI International Botanical Congress* at Missouri Botanical Garden, 1999.

Fredrickson, Ed, R. E. Estell, A. S. Laliberte, and D. M. Anderson. "Mesquite Recruitment in the Chihuahuan Desert: Historic and Prehistoric Patterns with Long-Term Impacts." *Journal of Arid Environments* 65 (2006): 185–93.

Gonzales, Karen Weston. "You Can't Keep a Good Tree Down." *Tucson Weekly*, November 14, 2002. www.tucsonweekly.com/tucson/you-cant-keep-a-good-tree-down/Content?oid=1071263

Haskell, David George. *The Songs of Trees: Stories from Nature's Great Connectors.* New York: Penguin Publishing Group, 2017.

———. Interview: *The Songs of Trees.* 2017. https://itunes.apple.com/do/book/the-songs-of-trees/id1142057908.

Hodgson, Wendy C. *Food Plants of the Sonoran Desert.* Tucson, AZ: University of Arizona Press, 2001.

Infuso, Barry, and Gary Nabhan. "Sweet and Spicy Mescal-Flavored Coleslaw." In Joe Yonan, ed., *America: The Great Cookbook.* New York: Weldon Owen in association with Blackwell & Ruth, 2017.

Keys, Roy N., Stephen L. Buchmann, and Steven E. Smith. "Pollination Effectiveness and Pollination Efficiency of Insects Foraging *Prosopis velutina* in Southeastern Arizona." *Journal of Applied Ecology* 32, no. 3 (1995): 519–27.

Kreiger, Alex D. *We Came Naked and Barefoot: The Journey of Cabeza de Vaca across North America.* Austin, TX: University of Texas Press, 2002.

Lewin, Alex, and Raquel Guajardo. *Kombucha, Kefir, and Beyond.* Beverly, MA: Fairwinds Press/Quarto Publishing, 2015.

Mancuso, Stefano, and Alessandra Viola. *Brilliant Green.* Washington, DC: Island Press, 2015.

Martin, Paul S. *Twilight of the Mammoths: Ice Age Extinctions and the Rewilding of America.* Berkeley, CA: University of California Press, 2007.

Martínez, Armando J., J. López-Portillo, A. Eben, and J. Golubov. "Cerambycid Girdling and Water Stress Modify Mesquite Architecture and Reproduction." *Population Ecology* 51 (2009): 533–41.

Massaad, Barbara Abdeni. *Mezze: A Labor of Love*. Beirut, Lebanon: Alwadi, 2014.

Micallef, Mike. *Reata: Legendary Texas Cuisine*. Berkeley, CA: Ten Speed Press, 2009.

Midwood, A. J., T. W. Boutton, Steve R. Archer, and S. E. Watts. "Water Use by Woody Plants on Contrasting Soils in a Savanna Parkland." *Plant and Soil* 205 (1998): 13–24.

Minckley, Robert L. List of bees and their floral hosts in the San Bernardino Valley of Arizona and Sonora, aka the Minckley Bee Table. 2000–2006. http://www.sas.rochester.edu/bio/labs/Minckley/minckley_table.php

Monroy-Ata, Arcadio, Juan Carlos Peña-Becerril, and Mariano García-Díaz. "Mycorrhizal Symbiosis Organization of Dominant Tree *Prosopis laevigata* (Mesquite) in a Xeric Scrub of Central Mexico." In M. C. Pagano, ed., *Recent Advances on Mycorrhizal Fungi*. Geneva, Switzerland: Springer International Publishing, 2016.

Moody, Mark, and Jesse Moody. "Arizona Mesquite Company." *Aridus* 21, no. 1 (2009):1–3.

Nabhan, Gary Paul. *Desert Terroir: Exploring the Unique Flavors and Sundry Places of the Borderlands*. Austin TX: University of Texas Press, 2011.

—— and John L. Carr, eds. *Ironwood: An Ecological and Cultural Keystone of the Sonoran Desert*. Washington, DC: Conservation International Occasional Papers in Conservation Biology/University of Chicago Press, 1994.

—— and Paul Mirocha. *Gathering the Desert*. Tucson, AZ: University of Arizona Press, 1985.

Niethammer, Carolyn. *Cooking the Wild Southwest: Delicious Recipes for Desert Plants*. Tucson, AZ: University of Arizona Press, 2011.

Okin, G. S., A. J. Parsons, J. Wainwright, J. E. Herrick, B. T. Bestelmeyer, D. C. Peters, and E. L. Fredrickson. "Do Changes in Connectivity Explain Desertification?" *BioScience* 9 (2009): 237–44.

Orozco-Villa Fuente, Juan, L. Buendía-Gonzalez, F. Cruz-Sosa, and E. J. Vernon-Carter. "Increased Mesquite Gum Formation in Nodal Explants Cultures After Treatment with a Microbial Biomass Preparation." *Plant Physiology and Biochemistry* 43, no. 8 (2005): 802–807.

Peattie, Donald Culross. *A Natural History of Western Trees*. Cambridge, MA: Riverside Press, 1953.

Rea, Amadeo M. *At the Desert's Green Edge: An Ethnobotany of the Gila River Pima*. Tucson, AZ: University of Arizona Press, 1997.

——— *Once a River: Bird Life and Habitat Changes on the Middle Gila*. Tucson, AZ: University of Arizona Press, 1993.

Rogers, Ken R. *The Magnificent Mesquite*. Austin, TX: University of Texas Press, 2000.

Savage, Sunny. *Wild Food Plants of Hawai'i*. CreateSpace Independent Publishing Platform, 2015.

Schmidt, Justin O. *The Sting of the Wild*. Baltimore, MD: Johns Hopkins University Press. Privately printed, San Bernardino, CA, 2016.

Schulter, Mary Elizabeth. "Disease and Curing in a Yaqui Community." In Edward Spicer, ed. *Ethnic Medicine in the Southwest*. Tucson, AZ: University of Arizona Press, 1934.

Simpson, Beryl B., and Jeffrey L. Neff. "Prosopis Flowers as a Resource." In Beryl B. Simpson, ed., *Mesquite: Its Biology in Two Desert Scrub Ecosystems*. Stroudsburg, PA: Dowden, Hutchinson and Ross, 1977.

———. "Pollination Ecology in the Arid Southwest." *Aliso* 11 (1987): 417–40.

Strange, Frances, and Terry Thompson-Anderson. *Don Strange of Texas: His Life and Recipes*. Fredericksburg, TX: Shearer Publishing, 2010.

Ulloa, M., and T. Herrera. "*Torulopsis taboadae*, una nueva especie de levadura aislada del colonche de Zacatecas, México." *Boletín de la Sociedad Mexicana de Micología* 12 (1978): 5–12.

Velasquez-Manoff, Moises. "Microbes: A Love Story." *New York Times,* February 12, 2017. https://www.nytimes.com/2017/02/10/opinion/sunday/microbes-a-love-story.html

Webb, George. *A Pima Remembers*. Tucson, AZ: University of Arizona Press, 1959.

Webb, Robert H., Julio L. Betancourt, R. Roy Johnson, and Raymond M. Turner. *Requiem for the Santa Cruz*. Tucson, AZ: University of Arizona Press, 2014.

Wohlleben, Peter. *The Hidden Life of Trees*. Vancouver, BC: Greystone Press with David Suzuki Institute, 2015.

INDEX

INDEX

INDEX

INDEX

ABOUT THE AUTHOR

Gary Paul Nabhan is an internationally celebrated nature writer, Franciscan contemplative, food and farming activist, and proponent of conserving the links between biodiversity and cultural diversity. He has been honored as a pioneer and creative force in the local food movement and seed-saving community by *Utne Reader, Mother Earth News,* Bioneers, *The New York Times,* and *Time* magazine. As the W. K. Kellogg Endowed Chair in Sustainable Food Systems at the University of Arizona Southwest Center, he works to build a more just, nutritious, sustainable, and climate-resilient foodshed spanning the US–Mexico border. He was among the earliest researchers to promote the use of native foods in preventing diabetes, especially in his role as a cofounder and researcher with Native Seeds/SEARCH. Gary is also personally engaged as an orchard-keeper, wild foods forager, and pollinator habitat restorationist, working from his small farm in Patagonia, Arizona, near the Mexican border. He has helped forge "the radical center" for collaborative conservation among farmers, ranchers, indigenous peoples, and environmentalists in the West. He played key roles in achieving the designations of Ironwood Forest National Monument and of Tucson as a UNESCO City of Gastronomy. He is also the author of numerous books, including *Growing Food in a Hotter, Drier Land, Renewing America's Food Traditions*, and *Chasing Chiles*. See www .garynabhan.com for notices of his speaking events and recent articles or forthcoming books.

About the Foreword Author

Petey Mesquitey (aka Peter Gierlach) is a native-plant grower, storyteller, and radio personality based in southern Arizona, and former lead singer for the legendary Dusty Chaps.

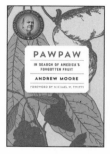
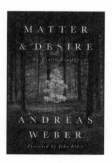
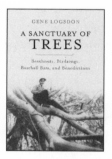